THE FABRIC
MAKES THE QUILT

Roberta Horton

C&T PUBLISHING

The Fabric Makes the Quilt
©1995 Roberta Horton

Front Cover: Collage of Roberta Horton's Quilts
Photography of Finished Quilts: Sharon Risedorph
All Other Photography: Roberta Horton
Editing: Louise Owens Townsend
Technical Editing: Joyce Engels Lytle
Book Design, Back Cover Design
   & Illustration: Jill K. Berry
Front Cover Design: Bobbi Sloan

Published by C&T Publishing, P.O. Box 1456, Lafayette, California 94549

Library of Congress Cataloging-in-Publication Data
   Horton, Roberta.
        The fabric makes the quilt / by Roberta Horton
            p.   cm.
        Includes bibliographical references (p.111).
        ISBN: 0-914881-98-1 (pbk.)
            1. Quilting. 2. Quilts—Design. 3.Textile fabrics in art
      I. Title.
      TT835.H625   1995
      7746.46—dc20   95-14001
                                          CIP

We wish to thank Wilanna Bristow for the use of her knotting method (Method B on page 106).

We have made every attempt to properly credit the trademarks and brand names of the items mentioned in this book. We apologize to any companies that have been listed incorrectly, and we would appreciate hearing from you.

   Chaco Liner chalk and Chacopel fabric marking pencils are products of Clover
      Needlecraft Inc.
   Featherweight is a trademark of The Singer Company
   Gammill handguided quilting machine is a product of Gammill Quilting Machine
      Company
   Nymo is a registered trademark of Belding Heminway Company, Inc.
   Perfect Sew wash-away fabric stabilizer is a trademark of Palmer/Pletsch
   Schmetz is a brand name of Ferd. Schmetz GmbH., Germany
   Sewer's Aid is a product of W.H. Collins, Inc.
   Sulky is a registered trademark of Sulky of America
   Versatex is a brand name of Versatex Company
   Vis-à-Vis overhead projector pen is a registered trademark of Sanford Corporation,
      a Newell Company

Printed in Hong Kong

10   9   8   7   6   5   4   3   2   1

TABLE OF CONTENTS

Dedication

Thanks to my father,
Peter Mashuta,
for being my biggest promotor
throughout the 25 years
of my quilting career.
You truly are
my sugar daddy.

Acknowledgments

I wish to thank all the quiltmakers who have contributed their quilts to this book. I appreciate your pushing forward through the travails of tendinitis, carpal tunnel, a broken shoulder, and pregnancy to meet my deadlines. I would also like to express a special thanks to the quiltmakers of Japan and South Africa who have really inspired me. And to the fabric makers of the world, Bravo!

A Zulu *sangoma* (right) and her apprentice (left) in Natal, South Africa. They are garbed in beautiful fabrics, richly adorned with wonderful beadwork. Photo: Roberta Horton

I believe that your quilts are a reflection of who you are, the time period in which you make them, and where you live. The world is truly getting smaller. Witness the wonderful international exchange between quiltmakers through our symposiums, books, and magazines. We learn from and inspire each other. And we all love fabric!

As a travelling quiltmaking teacher, I've had one of the greatest gifts—to be able to see other countries through the eyes of the people who live there. And a chance to buy their fabric.

In this book I have worked with fabrics from America, Africa, Australia, The Netherlands, Germany, Japan, and India. I have discovered that all fabrics, whatever their origin, have certain characteristics and qualities in common, although they may initially appear to be different. The purpose of this book is to share my discoveries, and also my thoughts, about fabric with you. Fabric has long been the inspiration for my quilts, and I have found that it has influenced how I make my quilts. Learning to read my fabric has made me more creative.

I have divided this book into five sections. First, I have attempted to explain creativity in my own words. Throughout the book I have tried to stress how each of us can be more creative. Next, in the Basics section, I have tried to reassess the foundation of our quiltmaking knowledge: color, value, and fabric pattern, design principles, and even the tools we use.

The Process chapter deals with all the ways we can use our fabric creatively as we build our quilts. Since many of the photo examples throughout the book come from my African Safari class, I also have added a Gallery section, which features quilts made in my Japanese Fabric Adventure class. The same creative principles and approaches were used to make these quilts. Once again, the fabric dictated our course of action. Finally, I have included a Techniques chapter, which includes more creative ways to approach our sewing tasks.

Have you ever had to change a quilt in midstream? Or wished that you had! Has a fabric behaved differently than you had expected? Did it seem lighter or darker, or even a different color when it was inserted in the quilt? Did it read too calm or too busy in relation to its neighbors? Most of us have had such an experience.

Some quilters don't bother to look at their quilt until it's finished because they are following a formula: find a pattern, select the fabric, cut, and sew. When they finish and then discover the troublesome fabric, they can be heard to say, "If I did it again, I would do thus and so...."

A second group of quiltmakers following the same formula looks at the quilt and makes changes, or adjustments, as work progresses. Sometimes the reason for the change can be identified; other times the quilter has a "feeling," which causes her to act in a certain way. Occasionally the fabric that inspired the quilt doesn't even end up in the quilt! So be it.

Think what would happen if the fabric itself told you what to do. All you had to do was to listen. What a relief! Well, my theory is that the fabric does indeed tell us what to do. With this book I propose to show you how to listen. And then what to do. How you can go from preformed blocks to free-form quilts....

What does it mean to be creative? How do you measure it? Finally, how can you be more creative? People have lots of questions about creativity, so many studies are being done and many books and articles are being written on the subject. I have purposefully not read them because I want to be able to discuss this subject based on my experiences as someone who both makes quilts and teaches others about quiltmaking.

In a workshop, there is often someone who comes up with more novel solutions than other participants. The rest of the class considers that person creative. Well, I believe that *everyone* is creative. Some individuals just seem to be naturally gifted with larger amounts. I also truly believe that you can become more creative as you learn to access your mind. I see it happen all the time. I know that I feel more creative than I was 25 years ago as a new quiltmaker.

What does it mean to be creative? The act of producing something is considered being creative. So, just making a quilt can make us creative. Personally, I feel that the more the decisions are yours as production evolves, the more creative you are. However, if the options all have been determined in advance by someone else, merely making the object—in this case a quilt—isn't a creative act.

I remember being thrilled as a child when I received a paint-by-number kit with the picture of a scene. I diligently worked at the project but it was never mine. It

didn't become a treasured family heirloom. The scene was already complete, the colors had been selected. I merely had to follow directions and apply the provided paint in the correct numbered areas.

The same lack of creativity would exist if you bought a kit for a quilt where the directions, fabrics, templates, even the quilting designs were supplied. You would merely be required to do the necessary labor. No choices would be required from you.

If you took the quilt kit and changed something, for example the quilting pattern, your project wouldn't look like all the others made from that kit. Another maker of the same kit upon seeing your change would be likely to comment, "Oh, I wish I had thought to do that. How creative you are."

Indeed, think how much more creative you would be considered if you made your own pattern and selected your own fabrics and quilting design. There would be much more satisfaction for you knowing that they were your own. The purpose of this book is to help you do these very activities.

Personally, I can tell when I'm being creative because everything just seems to flow. No matter what I do, it feels right. It's a magic place to be. Initially there may be a feeling of discovery or resolution, which may be accompanied by a statement like "Aha!" or "Oh!" or "Eureka!" I understand that flow has even become the official term used to describe the creative process. I tend

to make up words and for once my word is the right one.

Something to consider: As you master a subject, it seemingly takes a bigger challenge to feel creative. We all need to continue to try new things so that we can continue to grow and not become stale. There are charts in some of the following chapters showing how to "up the ante" as you move along in your quiltmaking career.

Creativity seems to have something to do with individual choices and interpretations. Extra points are awarded for imagination and inventiveness. While reading a quilt book in which the text had been translated into English I came across the word "inventivity." Although I'm sure that such a word doesn't really exist, I thought it sounded like a good quality to have when you're trying to be creative.

Think about this: I didn't save drawings my daughter had done in a commercial coloring book. I did save, and even framed, some drawings that were her originals. We prize originality. The same is true for quilts. Antique quilts that show originality command a higher price than those that are ordinary. Something such as making the scale bigger or smaller than expected for the hexagons in your Grandmother's Flower Garden, or finding a new way to arrange those hexagons can make all the difference. Such quilts are valued for their uniqueness by collectors.

In order to understand how to be creative, and/or how to become more creative, you need to understand the right and left brain and how they work. When you create a quilt, you use both. Sometimes you make a choice because you're following a rule—that is, you use your left brain. Other times, you make a choice without a conscious reason; you merely have a feeling. Following your intuition means you're using your right brain. Both methods can be used in quiltmaking. The more of the latter, the more original your quilt is likely to be.

The left brain is the neat-and-tidy part of you. It organizes, gives an item a name, counts, and tells time. It makes rules and then wants you to follow them. The left brain helps you to analyze as you proceed through the steps of making a quilt. It conducts the critiques at the crucial stages. The left brain summarizes and then draws conclusions. It can tell you why you did something. When you show a newly completed quilt to a friend and you point out all the things that you wish you had done differently, that's your left brain talking.

I can often identify people who are strongly left brain by how they behave in class. They reach for their rulers along with the graph paper. They stay exactly on the blue lines. Left-brainers want to have a pattern or rule to follow. They like to do what they've already done because it's safe. Having a finished product to show for their work is very important.

People who are strongly right-brain are creative, artistic, and often messy. Many times they can't tell you why they did something—it just felt right. They are intuitive. You can identify when you're in right-brain mode because you lose track of time and you get lost in your project. Right-brainers are eager to try new things. They are curious and like to experiment. The process is more

important than the product.

I can recognize right-brain people in class because they often seem to have difficulty when they work with graph paper. They're apt to draw their lines without the aid of a ruler; they in fact wish that the paper were plain. They are more likely to find it hard to draft a pattern. They are also more likely to have inappropriate tools, feeling that any old thing will do or can be made to work. This is because right-brainers lean toward improvising.

How do you make choices? Do you follow the rules? Or, do you follow your instincts, doing the thing that feels appropriate? Probably most of us do a combination of both. I try to follow the rules when I'm driving my car. My safety and that of others will be affected by my behavior. So I'm basically a left-brain driver. However in an emergency situation, where the rules may no longer apply, I may

have to switch to my right brain and improvise.

Human beings have both a right and a left brain. In many individuals, one side seems to be, or is, more dominant. As a quiltmaker, you need to use both sides of your brain. The task is to learn to better utilize the untapped part.

Watch people change the blade in a rotary cutter. Person A separates the individual pieces and places them in a line, first to last. The appliance is then reassembled by reversing the order. Person B lays the pieces in a pile, not paying attention to how the parts relate to each other. After changing the blade, the tool is put back together, often in a random order. Person A is following the correct procedure to get guaranteed results—a rotary cutter that works well. When changing the rotary cutter blade, the quiltmaker needs to be in left-brain mode. That is accomplished by being neat-and-tidy, that is, by working in a row. In other activities, you may need to be in your right-brain mode.

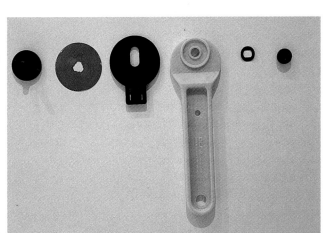

The left-brain approach to taking apart and reassembling a rotary cutter. Result: success

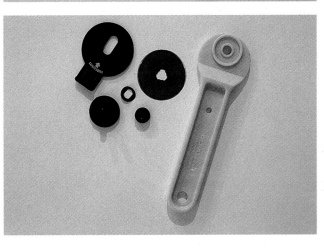

The right-brain approach to taking apart a rotary cutter. Result: chaos

When free-hand cutting a shape, which is a right-brain job, use plain paper. A lined writing paper or graph paper will present obstacles for the right brain, which equates lines with the bars of a jail cell. The lines will make your right brain a prisoner, not allowing it to do its job.

In order to access your right brain then, temporarily retire your graph paper and work only with plain paper. Turn off the television or radio, even the phone. I have recently discovered ear plugs! Remember, the right brain is non-verbal. Some very strong left-brain quilters may find that silence doesn't work for them. If this happens, try the opposite. Playing music can give the left brain something to do so that the right brain can come out to play. If one approach doesn't work, try the opposite.

I live with my sister Mary Mashuta who is also a quiltmaker. At breakfast one morning, she bemoaned the fact that she had a wonderful dream about a quilt. Upon waking, she immediately went to her studio. Getting out the graph paper, she attempted to capture the design, but was unable to do so. I suggested she try drawing the design on a piece of plain paper, which she was able to do. Of course it wasn't neat but she could then take that right-brain drawing and transfer it to graph paper so that she would have a more accurate left-brain plan to follow.

How can you be more creative? Here is a list of easy possibilities:

1. **Always present yourself with multiple choices.**
Through a process of elimination, you can determine the correct one.

2. **Try something that you haven't done before.**
Work with a new kind of fabric. Try a new design approach. Try a new technique.

3. **Allow a bigger block of time to work when you're in the creating stage of your quilt.**
You will have to think more and try some alternate solutions rather than just doing it the way you have always worked before.

4. **If you get blocked, do something unrelated to the quilt.**
Give your mind time to sort through the possibilities. I step out to my garden and deadhead flowers or harvest pesky snails. I take a nap or go to bed. You've heard the expression, "I have to sleep on it." It works. The solution is often freed while you're actively engaged in doing something else; it seems to just float up into your consciousness. It's commonly denoted in comic strips as a light bulb over someone's head.

5. **Learn to talk to yourself—and then to listen.**
I'll bet that you already do this but are reluctant to admit it to other people. I keep up a running commentary as I work. The first summer my sister and I shared our house, we had a common studio. Mistakenly thinking that I was talking to her, she keep saying, "What?" to me.

6. **Keep a plain paper notebook, or even the back of an envelope, handy.**
Writing material should be by your bed for when you wake up in the middle of the night. Those nocturnal ideas really do work, but if you don't jot them down, you won't remember them the next day. Sometimes, it's the thoughts you have when you first wake up in the morning that need to be captured.

7. **You may need to develop a new working-sleeping pattern.**
Many people find they work best late at night when there are no, or at least fewer, interruptions. My left brain seems to go to bed at 11 P.M. Some of my most creative thoughts have occurred to me around 1-2 A.M. I tend to get "slap-happy" (a silly or giddy condition). I try things I ordinarily wouldn't do. My mind seems to just hum along with these strange thoughts or solutions.

8. Think and talk in a positive fashion.

Many people think that they aren't creative, and they allow this belief to color their attitude about themselves, which is reflected in their quiltmaking. The trouble is that you listen to what you have to say about yourself. Consider what you're saying. Here are some examples:

Statement
"I can't."
Replacement Statement
"I'll try.

■

Statement
"I'm not good with...."
Replacement Statement
"I'm getting better at...."

■

Statement
"It's unlike me."
Replacement Statement
Thank goodness, this is different!"

9. Encourage and honor your creativity.

Artists often take their creativity for granted. The rest of us need to acknowledge ours. If you're having dreams and unsolicited thoughts about your project, your "inventivity" is at work.

Fabric

Ultimately I have decided that one of the greatest joys for me comes from acquiring fabric and then figuring out how to use it. New quiltmakers may be surprised to learn that the second step doesn't necessarily immediately follow the first. Sometimes I "save" a fabric because it's too precious to use. Now I know that you only truly know a fabric when you have cut into it. That incision seems to release the creativity woven within the threads. In other words, it's not enough just to own it.

I believe in having a well-rounded fabric collection, an array that gives me multiple choices in color, value, and visual pattern. Some of the fabrics are prominent and eye-catching; some of the fabrics are merely fill-ins, which assist us in seeing and appreciating the important fabrics. Consider this: Visually, some of the fabric in our quilts does nothing more than cover the batting!

There are two basic ways to look at fabrics. There are those fabrics that seem naturally to go together because they're similar. And, those that seemingly don't go together, because they're different. The first approach is the easiest, safest way, the road taken by many quiltmakers. It can also be boring. (Did you know that more vanilla ice cream is sold than any other flavor?) The second, mismatching approach is scary. I always recommend that if your first reaction is, "How awful!" your second reaction should be to say, "I'll try it."

On this page you'll see some traditional fabrics that I purchased in Germany. They look very much like American calicoes. Notice that I favored the navy, a favorite color of mine. When I went to use them, I discovered that all of my navies blended together.

I selected four for their mismatching qualities—both color and pattern. I had to add some lighter fabrics because even though I had different colors, the values were very similar. The lights are plaids and stripes because the rest are prints.

Traditional Fabrics Purchased in Germany

Fabric Palette for Block

The completed block may look much better than you assumed it would. The orange and pink that clashed in the fabric grouping actually look exciting in the finished Wonderful World block. Every piece of fabric has three characteristics that need to be considered: color, value, and pattern. Quiltmakers need to re-order their thinking so that they buy fabric that they need rather than just fabric that they like. Sometimes a fabric you dislike would really allow another favorite fabric to show even better. Let's take a look at each of the characteristics individually, remembering that they all add together to form any one fabric.

Wonderful World pattern by Judy Martin in her book, *Scraps, Blocks & Quilts*

Color

Color is the hue of the fabric. We all tend to have a favorite color that flavors our buying habits. Just inspect your fabric collection to bear this out. You feel comfortable with the colors you use the most. I maintain that you can't become good with a color unless you practice with it. Think about that!

Suffice it to say that you need examples of *all* the colors you can locate. Looking at the color wheel here, you will find some section that you ignore. On purpose buy some of the missing color. It may be that you buy only blue-greens. Pick up some yellow-greens, like avocado and chartreuse.

Truths About Color:

1. Every color is good. Each will do something that no other color will do. I've finally discovered the secret of yellow-green. It's so sour that it will make any other color look better. You need to operate at a level where you can impartially reach for a color because you know that it will work, not because it's a favorite.
2. Colors don't have to be used in equal amounts. One can be in the majority, the other in the minority or in an accent role.
3. Use colors together that mismatch so that they will read as individual pieces of fabric and not all mush together.
4. Don't worry about color schemes. Any combination goes together if you just repeat it.
5. The warm colors come toward you and the cool colors recede. Use this knowledge to give a feeling of depth.
6. The greater the number of colors on a fabric, the busier it will be perceived. The same is probably true for the quilt itself.

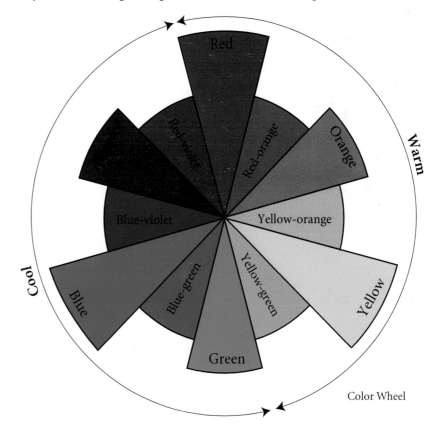

Color Wheel

Value

Value is the lightness or darkness of the fabric. Another way to say this would be, "Does a fabric most closely resemble white, gray, or black?"

Just as we have a favorite color, we also have a favorite value. Most quilters only buy two values, or at least they always seem to have less of

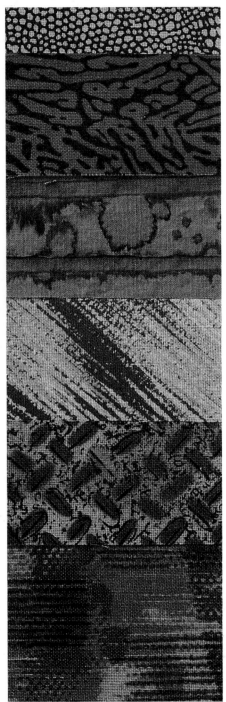

Texture Prints

one. People who favor lights never buy darks because they're depressing. People who wallow in their darks dismiss light as being pale, insipid, and boring. Where is your thermostat set? Value is a classic example of where you must go beyond your normal limits. Buy the missing value, and use it!

Truths About Value:

1. Value contrast establishes the visual image of what you see. Fabrics that are of like value will be perceived as one unit, regardless of color differences.
2. Value can establish depth. Usually light comes toward you, and dark recedes. The opposite can also be true. The dark can come toward you and the light can recede. You just need to know that the area with value contrast won't be read as flat.
3. Your eye goes to or follows white. Analyze its placement in your quilt. Used repeatedly, it can provide a visual pathway through your quilt.
4. Lighter objects read as larger. Darker objects read as smaller.
5. Fabric with a high value contrast between the background and the subject matter is usually harder to use because it's so eye catching. It takes over, and you can't see anything else. This is particularly true for large-scale prints. Pair high-value contrast prints with calmer, low-value contrast prints.

Pattern

The last characteristic of fabric is the pattern. After 25 years as a quiltmaker, I've finally figured out that all I need to know about any fabric is whether it's calm or busy. This determination will then

influence how I combine my focus or important fabrics with others.

Some prints are realistic; that is, they depict something that exists. Some fabric is stylized. This means that the shape may be recognizable but truly doesn't exist as a real object. You know that the design is a flower but it won't be in a botany book.

A useful category that has been added in recent years is texture. These are wonderful because they give us something to look at but we don't really have to focus on them as much as on a realistic or stylized print. They would normally be used in a secondary way, not detracting from the important or focus fabrics.

CALM	BUSY
solid	texture
solid	print
texture	print
small scale	large scale
geometric	floral
straight lines	curved lines
directional on grain	print
directional on grain	directional off grain

Summary:

When the time comes to make your fabric selections, the choice may be based on color, value, and/or pattern. When we have to make choices, our left brain springs into action. It lists the options, sorts through them, and makes a decision.

To audition fabric, lay it on a table or on the floor. If fabric is askew, raw edges exposed, stray threads floating over the surface, your left brain will be overwhelmed and you won't be able to make a choice.

The left brain sees everything! Give it only one choice. Make everything uniform. Remember, in order to access your left brain, you

Right-brain Fabric Arrangement

Left-brain Fabric Arrangement

will have to be neat and tidy. Therefore, lay your fabric out in rows with equal amounts exposed. Look at your project, and then peruse the choices that have been neatly arranged in front of you. Your eye will go right to the fabric you need.

A strong right-brain quilter can make a choice from fabric randomly spread all over the floor. Scanning the mess, her eye will alight on the proper choice—provided that it is visible—and her hand will reach for it. Such quilters happily accept intuitive choices but won't be able to tell you why they chose it. It's enough that the fabric works.

A word of caution: the left brain can be dictatorial. It can tell your nonverbal right brain that the "feeling" you have isn't the right answer. Those of you who are strongly left brain need to know that it's important to follow your urges. If your hand reaches for a fabric, try it. Don't talk yourself out of it. Left-brain quilters can talk an idea to death. Stop talking, and try it.

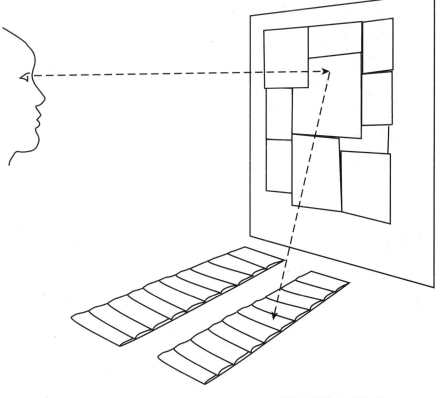

Work Wall: Auditioning

Design Principles and Concepts

Here are the principles and concepts that I have found the most helpful during my quilting career. I haven't attended art school so I have no idea if these are universally accepted truths. Some of my rules are so incredibly simple that I'm amazed it took me so many years to figure them out. No matter, here are my quiltmaking guidelines:

1. Repetition makes things go together.

I have already discussed this rule in terms of color. It also applies to design. Your eye will follow and collect similar items. The idea is to have the eye travel across the surface of your quilt.

Let's look at *Celebrate* by Jerry Kelley. The circle is the repeated element in this quilt. Printed circles march in an orderly fashion across the top border. In contrast, larger appliquéd circles spill in across the right-hand border fabric. A few more of the printed circles appear in the lower right-hand border. There are also four fish enclosed in gold circles in the center area. Circular motifs are featured on at least five other fabrics. The strong zigzag on the left and bottom border keeps the circles from being too overwhelming.

1. *Celebrate.* 42" x 42". Jerry Kelley, Nederland, Texas, 1993.

We can use repetition to select our quilting designs. Don't be afraid to recycle motifs found in the textiles used in the project. Janet Shore in *Stars of Africa* (Quilt 18, page 45) borrowed the star motif that already appeared in several of her fabrics. Don't fear that this is a too simple and easy solution. Instead, you will achieve continuity through the repetition. Examine the orange, red, and green stripes in Janet's quilt for the quilted stars.

2. It's important that the line isn't straight.

I once heard a lecture given by Ed Larson that had this title. It was a mind-altering thought for me. I have always been drawn to folk art, partially for its unpretentiousness. Among antique quilts, it's frequently not the quilt with the best workmanship that wins my heart. I more often am attracted to the quirky ones. However, it's one thing to appreciate crooked lines in someone else's work and then be able to take the next step and do it myself. After all, I was trained as a home economics teacher, and I know how it's supposed to be.

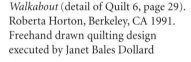

Sometimes it's a matter of not seeing, or acknowledging, what is really there. I am fascinated with Australian Aboriginal art. Some styles feature the use of multiple lines to fill in the background. I realized that I could use this idea when designing the quilting for my solid

Walkabout (detail of Quilt 6, page 29). Roberta Horton, Berkeley, CA 1991. Freehand drawn quilting design executed by Janet Bales Dollard

color spaces in *Walkabout*. Initially I got out my quilter's ruler and began to draw lines in a tidy fashion. No, that wasn't what I had seen! The lines were crooked—they were neither straight nor were they parallel. I needed to draw the lines free-hand to accomplish the correct look. Study the quilting in the borders of *Walkabout*.

At left is a piece of fabric I purchased in Africa, which featured linear strips. Studying the third design from the left side, you can see that it would be possible to cut out that strip using a ruler. However, a lot of the rust color would be lost to the straightening process, resulting in a very narrow strip.

Instead, I decided to go with the fabric. I cut it with scissors, adding on a seam allowance at the line where the color changed. Because of the randomly curved sewing line, I found it easiest to hand appliqué the brown strip onto some gray fabric. The resulting composition was then cut into a straight strip for ease in piecing. Locate five strips that were handled in this fashion in Quilt 27 on page 59.

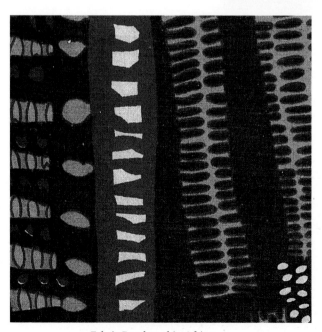

Fabric Purchased in Africa

Don't Center.

3. Don't center.

Americans tend to work in a symmetrical framework. I've always said that if you gave an American two candlesticks and a fireplace, she could perfectly arrange the candlesticks on opposite ends of the mantle, equidistant from the center. This tendency towards symmetry is part of the European design heritage that pervades our culture.

Well, there are alternate solutions. A Japanese solution for the above scenario would be to take the candlesticks and arrange them in an asymmetrical placement. Once you have mastered being symmetrical, try the opposite. I know that it's very comfortable, not to mention safe, to be symmetrical because that's what we're used to seeing and doing. It also doesn't require much thinking. I believe that it's a too-easy solution.

One major disadvantage of a symmetrical arrangement is that the eye becomes focused in the middle of the quilt rather than moving across the surface. You're held prisoner in the center. I call it the "belly button" syndrome. You're sucked into the middle and can't get out!

Let's look at *My Sister's Lament* by Linda Atkinson. The first stage shows the elephant batik panel at

Above: *My Sister's Lament* (in progress). First Stage: Symmetrical

Right: 2. *My Sister's Lament.* 36" x 45". Linda Atkinson, Indianapolis, Indiana, 1993.

dead center. The fish are the "candlesticks." The top and bottom borders match. As the quilt became larger, the batik elephant dropped below the center point of the quilt, breaking away from the symmetrical arrangement. The original two fish were shifted, and a third was added in another panel. Additional elements were added to the composition. Little "confetti" shapes have been added (See Rule #4 below). The last step was the addition of the borders. Notice that they aren't one equal width nor has one uniform fabric been used. All of the selected fabrics already appear in the quilt.

Keep the eye moving.

4. Keep the eye moving.

It's important to develop a rhythm or movement in your quilt. Static quilts are uninteresting and safe. Consider the arrangement of important colors or shapes. Rather than lining up similar important shapes/colors in a row, consider alternative arrangements where they move through the quilt.

Refer to *Stars of Africa* (Quilt 18, page 45). Janet Shore placed the stars in a random fashion rather than superimposing them on top of the printed strips. This makes the stars appear to float across the surface, which keeps the eye moving. In *My Sister's Lament,* Linda Atkinson used small shapes to integrate the quilt into a whole. Linda's "confetti" happened to be a mixture of circles, squares, and elephants that she found printed on fabric. Confetti shapes can also be cut from solid fabrics in a selection of eye-catching colors. I also sometimes call these units "band-aids."

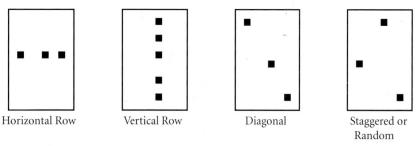

| Horizontal Row | Vertical Row | Diagonal | Staggered or Random |

| Static Arrangement | | Movement Arrangement | |

If it's too big, cut it off.
If it's too small, add onto it.

5. If it's too big, cut it off. If it's too small, add onto it.

Here's a practical solution to many problems. How simple can you get? I first recognized this approach as a viable solution while studying African-American quilts. Now I readily see evidence of this technique in many antique quilts, particularly in utility quilts.

This rule is the basis for how I now make quilts. It's so important a concept that I will discuss it fully later in "The Process" section of this book (Chapter 3). In the meantime, just salt away the idea, and let your brain absorb it. Right now, study Cynthia Corbin's *Masks* (following page). It's a good example of this approach. Cynthia worked with a collection of Japanese textiles placed in rows.

6. A quilt must be big enough to say something.

My quilts tend to be all different sizes. I never know when I start a project exactly what the finished size will be. Sometimes I'm limited by the amount of yardage of the fabrics I am using. More importantly, though, there seems to be an inherent right size for each project. There has to be enough to look at to make a statement.

The scale of the design on the fabric itself can to be an important factor in determining the finished size of a quilt. If you're truly paying attention to your fabric, you will find that large-scale fabric usually needs a larger canvas to be seen than small-scale fabric. There has to be enough subject matter, or fabric showing, to tell a story. One problem with miniature quilts is that they don't let us see very much of the fabric. Or you're restricted to using only small-scale fabrics so that entire motifs can be seen.

When working with a traditional pieced block, I will draw the block in several different sizes. I don't look at the finished size of the block itself but at the smallest and largest template shapes within the block. I then think about how much of my fabric could show in that space. Enough of the important fabrics must be viable to influence how I behave. If I were to cut everything up like spaghetti, what difference would any one fabric make?

My advice is to start saying, "Let's see what happens." Don't feel that all quilts must be bed-sized in order to be correct. Judy Hopkins' *Avis Afrikanus* is only 19½" x 21", but I feel that this small wall hanging is a complete composition. There's enough happening visually to keep you occupied for a long time.

Let's analyze why *Avis Afrikanus* breaks my common-sense rule about scale. Remember that I said that using

3. *Masks.* 40" x 64". Cynthia Corbin, Woodinville, Washington, 1991. A Japanese fabric quilt made in rows

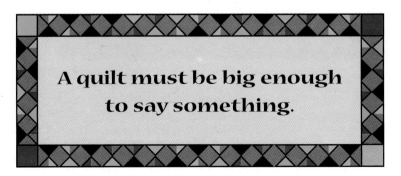

A quilt must be big enough to say something.

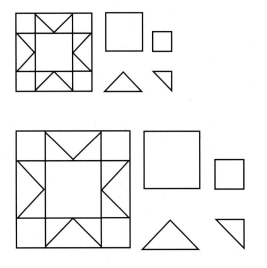

Pattern in two sizes

large-scale fabrics should mean that you make a large-scale quilt. The best things happen when you're able to break a rule, so let's see how it was accomplished:

First, notice that the central bird motif occupies a large proportion of the quilt. Its shape extends into the border, which allows the quilt's size to be smaller than if the bird had been more traditionally enclosed in a frame.

Secondly, the size of the bird was "set" by the fact the fabric was used as it was printed. The "wing" was part of an abstract design, not an appliquéd addition. Judy merely saw the potential for a bird in the fabric.

In the third place, a collage of fabrics other than traditional muslin (a plain solid) was used for the background. Thus a rich visual feast has been created by the variety of textural patterning and color.

And, finally, the borders present even more patterns to absorb. Notice the repetition of the zigzag motif at the top and bottom of the quilt. This adds a stabilizing influence.

4. *Avis Afrikanus.* 19½" x 21". Judy Hopkins, Anchorage, Alaska, 1993. A small quilt that's big enough to say something!

Tools

As a creative quiltmaker, it helps to be aware of the tools and equipment available to you. This is always changing, so periodically survey the market and "take a test drive." A reason for making one of my recent quilts was so that I could try all the new bonding agents that have been created for machine appliqué. I also wanted to try out some of the beautiful new threads that are now on the market.

Oddly enough, some of the tools available to us have made us less creative; they can limit our creativity if we're not careful. Some of the tools were invented specifically for quiltmakers, or at least, were first utilized as a quilting tool during this revival. Looking over the chart below, I see that the tools are left-brained in the sense that they allow us to be more perfect and exact. Remember: When we operate like a machine, we become less creative. However, these tools can all be used in a right-brain way, too.

> ## Some Tools To Re-evaluate:
> ## PATTERNS
> ## QUILTERS' RULER
> ## ROTARY CUTTER
> ## GRAPH PAPER
> ## FREEZER PAPER
> ## DUPLICATING MACHINE

 Patterns First of all, there always seem to have been patterns. I encourage you to alter a pattern to make it your own. Use a pattern merely as a starting place. For example, try free-hand cutting the shape, using the pattern as an inspiration (Don't say, "I don't know how to do that." or "I can't do that." Refer to page 99). Chances are that your shape won't be a perfect duplicate of what you were copying. That's the whole point. Its inaccuracies make it unique—make the pattern yours.

 Quilters' Rulers Give a quiltmaker a quilters' ruler, a rotary cutter and mat, and some fabric, and she will obediently cut the fabric in a pre-selected, equally wide strip the width of the fabric. But consider this: It's also possible to take this same tool and to use it to cut a strip that goes from narrow to wide. We have choices: The ruler can be used just as a straight-edge where we ignore the printed lines, or we can use the ruler lines to measure prescribed widths. The trick is to know that you have both options, and when to use each one.

Hint: Right-brainers need to look at the quilters' ruler they're using. When selecting the ruler for measuring widths, choose a ruler that features heavier lines at the 1" intervals. You'll find these are easier to read than those with uniformly thick lines across the width of the ruler.

Rotary Cutter Most quiltmakers associate rotary cutters with quilters' rulers. Remember that a rotary cutter is merely a device to cut fabric and that it is used in much the same way as you would use scissors. It's possible to "carve" out an appliqué motif or a free-hand cut shape. Remember to make it a little bigger if you need a seam allowance.

Hint: You may find that you can execute curves more easily with the small size rotary cutter.

Graph Paper Graph paper is a real aid when you're trying to accurately draft a pieced pattern. You must also know when not to use graph paper. If you're exploring an idea, remember to work with plain paper because it's your right brain that's doing the creating.

When I demonstrate how to free-hand cut a shape, it's always the left-brain student who announces she can't do it. Just having my students switch to plain paper enables them to perform. The right-brain will get lost in all those lines and not be able to complete the image. Taking graph paper away from a left-brain person will make him or her initially feel insecure. However, it's a necessary step to allow access to the right brain.

Hint: If you have difficulty using graph paper, you're probably right-brained. I suggest that you purchase the kind of graph paper that has heavy dark lines at the inch intervals. The darker lines help you to keep your place as you work. Start drawings on these thicker lines.

Freezer Paper I began my quiltmaking career as an appliquér. I loved the freedom of appliqué as opposed to the rigidity of piecing. I thought that the shape was supposed to evolve as you sewed it. That was part of the fun.

Now, left-brainers have made appliqué into an art form where perfect replication seems to be the goal. When working with freezer paper patterns, it's possible to exactly duplicate a shape one time or many times. Why can't the leaves in a wreath, for example, all be slightly different? Why must they be a perfect match to each other? Remember, that's not how it is in nature.

I can see using freezer paper if it makes it easier for you to appliqué an individual shape, particularly if it's a small one. But please don't use it for endless repeated perfect duplication! And especially not if it's someone else's pattern that you are copying, as everyone else is also copying that same pattern. You don't want your quilt to look like preprinted cheater cloth.

Duplicating Machine Duplicating machines take the fun out of enlarging. If you do it yourself (see page 100), you're more likely to come up with an inaccurate rendition. Remember, then it will be more yours.

Duplicating machines can be used in very creative ways, as witness all the quilts that use images reproduced and then transferred onto fabric. The more creative users play with the machine dials and distort the image. Or they color the image with fiber paints. There are countless possibilities. Even though the images were reproduced by a machine, the artist somehow makes them her own.

Have you ever analyzed how you personally go about making a quilt? As I discuss the process I would like you to try, I want you to keep in mind two things. First, make your quilt for the joy of exploration and discovery, not for someone else's rules. Second, when thinking in terms of becoming more creative, no single quilt is important—only how it influences the next one you make.

Today there seem to be two categories of quilts being constructed. I call the first type a *generated* quilt. There is a formula that tells you the pattern, how many fabrics you need, what their color and value needs to be, a cutting scheme that includes the quantity in each group, and finally a sewing attack plan. When you've gone through the preceding steps you will at last find out what your quilt looks like.

At the opposite end of the spectrum exists the second type, which I call a *composed* quilt. This method of working involves minimal preplanning. The quilt comes mainly from the fabric itself. At its inception, the finished size is unknown. The quilt will come out the size it needs to be, based on how much fabric there is and what happens with that fabric as you move through the process.

I realize that the procedure you use to make a quilt may fall somewhere in between these two examples. For the purposes of this book, I want to explore the idea of composed quilts because all the solutions are ultimately dependent on the fabric, which is the subject of this book.

During the summer of 1986, I made two surprising discoveries. First, I could combine piecing and appliqué in one quilt, using whichever technique most easily accomplished the task at hand. I had been a quiltmaker long enough that I now could think both as an appliquér and as a piecer. Second, I didn't have to work in blocks, or even in the more liberating concept of rows.

The Long Hot Summer was inspired by watching a television dramatization of that name set in the southern United States. I had long wanted to do a quilt about the South, since my mother had been born in Mississippi. Architecture is a hobby of mine, so I'm very interested in that

Original Sketch, *The Long Hot Summer*

5. *The Long Hot Summer.* 46" x 49". Roberta Horton, Berkeley, California, 1987. Quilted by Janet Bales Dollard. A quilt meant to catch the aura of the South

region's beautiful antebellum houses. The closing scene in the television drama, which was filmed on a front porch, suddenly gave me a vision of how I could capture the feeling of such a house without actually having to replicate the entire structure. I made a quick little sketch and filed it away until I could work on the quilt.

The quilt evolved from my sketch. From my fabric collection, I auditioned possible column candidates, finally selecting a commercially produced tie-dye looking fabric. Fortunately, I had a yard of it, so that established the height of the quilt. The coloration of that fabric suggested the addition of roses to encircle the column. The roses were positioned to enhance the stained and/or shadowed area. I wanted to evoke a feeling of abundant vegetation and of hot, humid air.

The movie scene had been shot at night so I decided on the use of a variety of blacks and dark blues for the background. Pieced stars seemed appropriate. Notice that there's a coloration change in some of the star points. These were cut from the magic fabric that ultimately became the right and left borders. The red triangles, which were meant to suggest the fire in the story, were cut from the same color-changing fabric. Bow Tie blocks were worked into the porch area because two pivotal characters in the movie wore bow ties. Working in such a free-form way felt wonderful. Each time I held an audition for a particular fabric, I was able to recognize the "right" choice. The correct fabric spoke to me.

In 1990, I visited Australia for the first time. I fell in love with the Northern Territory. I loved the colors of the land and the art of the indigenous people. An important mission was to collect fabrics designed in Aboriginal ventures. The fabrics were produced in a variety of ways: silk screen, batik, and commercial printing.

The Tiwi men and women of Bathurst Island produce silk-screened fabrics. The men are also wood carvers. Their handiwork was

Top: Uluru (Ayers Rock), Northern Territory, Australia. (All photos on this page by Roberta Horton)

Middle: Aboriginal rock paintings, Kakadu National Park, Northern Territory, Australia

Bottom: Metal ceiling painted by the Tiwi of Bathurst Island, Northern Territory, Australia

Above: 6. *Walkabout*.
76" x 50". Roberta Horton,
Berkeley, California, 1991.
Quilted by Janet Bales
Dollard and Roberta Horton.
A quilt inspired by the
author's visit to Australia

Right: The beginning stage of
quilt composition for
Walkabout. The author used
the Aboriginal fabrics,
baskets, and ditty bags
collected on the trip for
inspiration and color
referencing

displayed in a metal building, the ceiling of which became the basis for *Walkabout*. The beginning stage photo was taken soon after I began the quilt. The ditty bags and baskets were collected to document colors. You'll notice that some fabrics made it to the final cut and others were eliminated.

Let's look at the top three rows on the upper right of *Walkabout*. They're arranged pretty much as I eventually sewed them. The second row had the most seams and would be the hardest to guess the finished width when sewn. Do you see that I had more flexibility in the width of individual segments in the rows directly above and below this row?

Eventually there were three segments of varying size that comprised the quilt. Since this composition looked too long and skinny, I added a fourth section that spanned the bottom. Now the quilt felt big enough to be something.

There's a lot of repetition of fabric in *Walkabout.* Looking at the quilt, I would realize that it was about time for a particular pattern or color to reappear. I was able to use nine free-hand cut blocks that enclosed the figures (refer to Techniques: Piecing on page 88). All but the smallest fragment of the 12" square of batik that started this enterprise was used.

Here was yet another quilt that literally made itself. I didn't always get to do what I wanted, either. Some important fabrics got left out for the improvement of the whole composition. Oh well, someday, in another quilt....

Here, then, are the steps in the design process as I have refined them over the ensuing years. As you will see from descriptions of quilts later in this book, these steps in the design process don't always develop in the same numerical order. For example, Numbers 8, 11, and 13 are covered in Chapter 5 as part of the techniques section.

Design Process

1. Inspiration
2. Collecting and selecting possible fabrics
3. Arranging fabric in rows by categories
4. Placing important fabrics on design wall
5. Looking at the fabric
6. Selecting a format
7. Composing quilt (auditioning fabrics)
8. Figuring out how to sew it all together
9. Auditioning, selecting, and attaching borders
10. Composing the backing
11. Creating quilting patterns and the quilting
12. Selecting and attaching binding
13. Embellishment if necessary
14. Labeling the quilt

Inspiration

"In creating, the hardest part is to begin." Anonymous.

I read this statement in a newspaper long ago. As you can see, I get turned onto wanting to make a quilt very easily. Sometimes it's triggered by attending an event, like a quilt show, or by a trip to an interesting place. Other times, it's a visit to the fabric store and the purchase of some fabric. It even can be so innocent a thing as running my hands over the fabrics stacked on the shelves in my studio. The desire is the easy part.

Collecting and Selecting Possible Fabrics

The author's first African fabrics collected in the United States

The actual starting can be tricky. I often try a neutral, non-threatening, approach. For example, I wash my new fabric, ironing it if necessary. Just the handling of the yardage in a non-committal way allows me to get to know the fabric better. The wheels begin to turn.

Placing Important Fabrics on the Design Wall

When I'm working with already owned and washed fabric, I move along to the next step. I go through my cupboards and pull out fabrics that might work in this quilt. I sort them into some kind of categories, which might relate to color, value, and design. Sometimes these piles are on the floor; other times I pin fabrics up on my design wall so I can see them better. I would particularly want to see any pivotal or very important fabrics up on my wall.

The photo here shows the first grouping of African fabrics I was able to amass. The right-hand two rows were fat-quarter segments; the seven vertical strips were in my preferred quantity of half-yard pieces.

Looking at the Fabric

I stared at this assortment for three weeks before making my first incision. Usually the "looking stage" is not nearly so long, lasting anywhere from a few hours to several days. In this case I was totally overwhelmed by the colors, the large scale, and the boldness of the designs. Still not knowing what I wanted to do, I finally made the daring move of cutting into some of the fabric and sewing it together. The following truths were revealed to me:

1. Many of the fabrics were in a narrow color range of yellow, rust, and black. This was particularly true in the case of the fat quarters, which had been marketed as preselected sets. I did a better job of mismatching, that is in having a variety of colors, in the ½ yard lengths I had selected independently.

2. The rust, yellow, and black dyes were basically identical in each piece of fabric. The rust matched the rust, the yellow matched the yellow. One's first reaction might be, "How wonderful, they match!" The problem is that they also "mushed." In some third world countries, it's too costly to have many different versions of each color. This sameness in color makes it difficult to differentiate one fabric from another. Sewing several triangles together proved this to me. The result read like one big square rather than four separate triangles.

3. Because of the largeness of scale, I needed to work with larger pieces of fabric. Fat quarters were almost useless. I needed at least ½-yard pieces; sometimes a yard was better. Fabrics that might serve as borders or backgrounds might even require 1½ to 2 yards.

4. I eventually figured out that the fabric could be divided into categories such as small and large scale, straight and curved lines, geometrics and florals, and all-over patterns and repeated motifs. But then I realized that these were the same categories I use for all my fabrics! So I had to refine the thought even further. What I needed were the words calm and busy! (See page 16.)

Arranging Fabric in Rows by Categories

This time, I had to do Steps 4 and 5 (page 30) to get to Step 3 in the design process. Now I had a handle on my fabric. Rearranging my fabric in neat rows according to the categories allowed me to see what else I needed. Before I could begin the composing stage, I had to make a fast run to the fabric store to buy

$100 worth of fabric now that I finally understood what I needed. I was in flow! By the way, seven of the original fabrics were eventually used in *Ishmail's Revisited* (Quilt 12, page 38) and ten were used in *Sangomas, Cocks, and Hens* (Quilt 21, page 49).

You'll notice that I didn't start my exploration of African fabric with graph paper, colored pencils, and ruler and then proceed to draft my quilt. That would be the left-brain way. Don't plan and talk it to death. Try to get to the fabric part as soon as possible. You want your quilt to evolve from your fabric. Remember, it's going to tell you what to do.

Louise Colbert had this to say, "I had never used this technique of pinning the various pieces of fabric onto the wall, moving and changing and replacing them until the quilt began to assert itself. What a marvelous technique this is! I have used it several times since and find that it frees me from 'tradition' and constraint and lets something inside come out and express itself." (Louise's quilt is No. 47, page 92.)

Selecting a Format

Many quilters work in the repeat block format because it's a tried and true quiltmaking formula to follow. Basically all you have to do is find a pattern, select some fabric, then commence cutting and sewing. Unfortunately, unusual fabrics don't always show to their best advantage when they are all sliced up into geometric shapes. The resulting quilt is often more static and controlled than the fabric promises.

I think that we need to explore some other directions that you might take when you want to build a quilt. Fortunately, there are alternative approaches that lend themselves to free-form solutions.

Probably the easiest format to use when you compose a quilt is to work with a background fabric that will serve as a canvas for your picture. I'm reminded of those children's story books with the slick cardboard pages and the plastic cutouts of shapes that will temporarily adhere to the pages. You can compose your own scenario as you mix and rearrange the shapes.

Ruth Harris named her quilt *Bonwire* (shown here) after the village where the first *kente* cloth was woven. She used a splotchy hand-dyed fabric as a background onto which she could erect a village scene. The background fabric needed to be lighter than the appliqué shapes so that there was sufficient contrast for the subject matter to be seen. At the same time, the background also needed to have enough color that the scene didn't appear to float. I would recommend auditioning several different pieces of fabric until you find the fabric with the right value or "guts quotient" for your composition. Notice how the vegetation placed throughout the village helps to unify the scene.

Jackie Carley took a three-day African Safari workshop with me. She gave the following testimonial, "On the first day, I worked on a piece that wasn't going anywhere. That night I awoke from a dream singing 'The Lion Sleeps Tonight.' I remembered a piece of fabric with lions on it that I had in my fabric collection. I jumped out of bed, went to my workroom and pulled fabric from shelves until I found *the* fabric. The next two days of the workshop breezed by as the quilt designed itself, thanks to a special fabric. I really do think the fabric makes the quilt!" Jackie's *The Lions Sleep Tonight* is shown here. Look carefully

7. *Bonwire.* 42" x 36". Ruth Harris, Fairfax Station, Virginia, 1994.

8. *The Lions Sleep Tonight.* 39" x 27". Jacquelin Carley, Anchorage, Alaska, 1994.

Opposite page: 9. *Ester—A Tribal Star.* 45" x 68". Tracy Allen, Pacheco, California, 1993.

Above: Ester Mahlangu of the Ndebele tribe, South Africa. She is wearing the traditional *ikumbesi,* a multi-colored wrapped blanket, and *iindzila,* neck rings. Ester is the artist who painted the building behind her. (Photo by Roberta Horton)

for the lions hidden in the green background fabric. They aren't visible from across the room, which adds to the fun of discovery.

Ester—A Tribal Star by Tracy Allen was inspired by photos of Ester Mahlangu, a member of the Ndebele tribe of South Africa. Tracy used Japanese *yukata* cloth for the background of her quilt. The traditional fabric is printed in only 14" widths, which can sometimes be a disadvantage. Tracy used this limitation to her advantage. She pieced in strips of printed *kente* cloth designs to camouflage the seams. Notice that these strips provide an interesting division of the background area.

Dena Canty was given a very special African batik fabric, which sat on her shelves for more than 10 years (see the photo on page 36 for the remaining fragment, which will give you an idea of the scene). This is the type of fabric that is really hard to cut into because you're afraid of ruining it—even if you have two yards. An alternate solution to cutting would be to patch onto it, which is the direction Dena took.

You must make the fabric yours. How many additions can you find in Dena's *African Vista* on page 36? She used both brown and blue batiks for her animal patches. The addition of huts helps to enhance the feeling of depth. Placing some green on the trees provides a welcome accent of color. Did you notice that Dena opted not to center the tree? The printed borders are visually complex, seeming to be intricately pieced. Their varied width helps to off-center the composition. Notice how the elephant intrudes onto the left border.

Sylvia Pressacco has opted in *Zebra* (on page 37) to collage a background. The four fabrics are of similar color and value. In this case, the background is darker than the subject matter, which happens to be light. Usually the reverse is true. The important concept is to strive for value contrast between the background and the subject matter. Notice that there isn't a traditional border on the right side of this quilt. The green pineapple stripe fabric forms a visual interruption in the background, which then continues to the edge. This green stripe serves to counterbalance the green border on the left-hand side.

This same approach to collaging a background can be used in a single block. Linda Atkinson used several different beige fabrics cut into random geometric shapes to create the interesting background for her fish in the upper right-hand corner of *My Sister's Lament* (page 37).

Remaining fragment of batik fabric given to Dena Canty

10. *African Vista.* 58" x 47". Dena Canty, Piedmont, California, 1994.

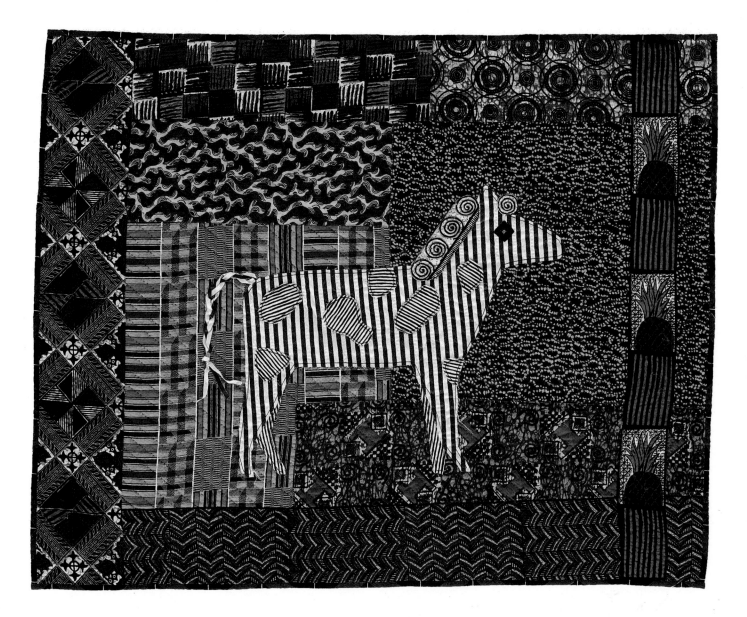

Above: 11. *Zebra*. 42" x 34". Sylvia Pressacco, Menlo Park, California, 1994.

Right: *My Sister's Lament* (detail of Quilt 2, page 20). Linda Atkinson, Indianapolis, Indiana, 1993.

Remember design rule 5 on page 21: **If it's too big, cut it off. If it's too small, add onto it.**
I must say that this is one of my favorite rules. Acknowledging it as a legitimate design principle really freed me in terms of quilt construction. The other three formats I want to discuss are all based on this thought. Working in vertical and horizontal rows or in sections presents a refreshing change from the tried-and-true repeat block checkerboard, but there is still the security of knowing that there are areas of containment.

Opposite page: 12. *Ishmail's Revisited.*
57" x 73". Roberta Horton, Berkeley,
California, 1992. Quilted by George Taylor.

Left: *Ishmail's Revisited.* First Stage

Below left: *Ishmail's Revisited.* Horizontal
and Vertical Rows

Below center: *Ishmail's Revisited.* Quilt
"Guts" Sewn Together

Below right: *Ishmail's Revisited.* Version I

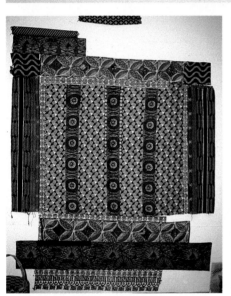

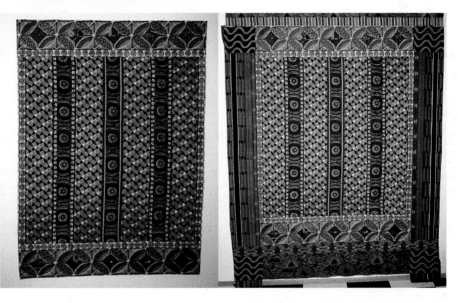

Ishmail's Revisited was named after the fabric store I visited in Johannesburg, South Africa. I remember being overwhelmed with the exotic fabrics—colors and designs seemed to leap off the wall at me. Because of a very drastic luggage restriction and due to my inexperience with such fabric, I purchased only modest amounts. Well, those walls of color and design haunted me in my dreams. Finally I decided that I was ready to tackle such wild fabric.

Here is the process I went through to create *Ishmail's Revisited.* Remember that this was after the three-week investment of time spent staring at my fabric collection that I mentioned earlier on page 31. The pictures above are ones I took as I moved along so that later I could go back and study them in a left-brain way to see where the insights had occurred. When asked specific questions about their quilts, right-brainers often say, "I don't know. It just happened."

1. My first breakthrough was when I realized that I could present the fabric in horizontal rows.
2. The red circle fabric wanted to be positioned vertically.
3. My thoughts about the center area were resolved adequately enough that I felt confident to sew that section of the quilt. Sometimes it's helpful to momentarily stop and straighten things up before going onto the next step. I refer to this as "cleaning up my act."
4. Now I could get back to fiddling with the borders. I auditioned two alternatives to the placement of the black/yellow serpentine fabric.

Technically I worked both vertically and horizontally in *Ishmail's Revisited.* The important thought is that at least it wasn't in a repeat block format. The finished quilt was an opportunity for me to just wallow in the richness of the fabric.

VERTICAL ROWS

Judy Huddleston in *Three Days and Thirteen Changes* worked in three vertical rows, separated by two sashes. Here is an in-progress picture, shot during the workshop, along with the finished quilt. You might already have guessed from Judy's selection of a title that there was a certain amount of fine tuning before she got the quilt resolved to her satisfaction. The biggest difference took place along the bottom border where there has been an important fabric change and the addition of some critters. How many more changes can you spot?

Left: *Three Days and Thirteen Changes* (in progress)

Below: 13. *Three Days and Thirteen Changes.*
44" x 34".
Judy Huddleston, Portland, Oregon, 1994.

14. *African Magic.* 40" x 51".
Helen Streit, Davis, California,
1994.

Helen Streit also worked in vertical rows in *African Magic*. She used seven strips of fabric to create the background. The fabric on the right looks like two sewn rows, but the fabric was merely printed in an off-set pattern. Notice that the free-hand cut Log Cabins and the figures float across the surface, not being trapped in one row. In Judy Huddleston's quilt (shown on facing page), the figures are restricted to their own rows except in the bottom border.

HORIZONTAL ROWS

African Tapestry by Christine Davis is made from horizontal rows. Each strip seems to have its own personality. The palm tree is the only object that goes over more than one seam but then perhaps the black/red stars, the houses, and the bordered serpentine strip all count as one row. The top row and the orange-red row were pieced but could have been cut from a large-scale striped fabric. The row featuring the diamonds is a printed fabric. The quilt didn't need a framing border fabric.

Christine had the following to say, "Working in rows like this was a very 'freeing' experience for me. It allowed me to concentrate on the individual units I was creating and

15. *African Tapestry.* 39" x 40". Christine Davis, Redmond, Washington, 1993.

then intuitively build a whole from them. All of the figures—the houses, the ladies, the animals, tree, symbols, *etc.*, are my own designs. They evolved after seeing Roberta's African slides. I also tried to let the fabric I was working with suggest what it would."

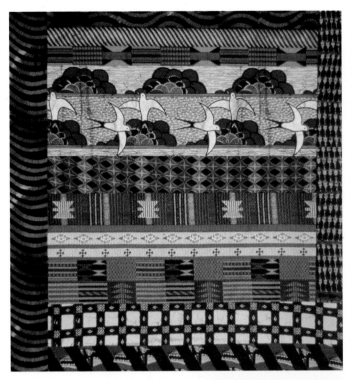

Because George Taylor used fabrics from Côte D'Ivoire, he decided to name his quilt *Sterne*, which is the French translation for tern, a coastal bird. Here is an in-progress shot of the original composition along with the completed quilt. Let's compare the two photos to see what changes were made to the final composition.

1. The second fabric from the bottom was printed off-grain. Trees have been added both on the upper left and the lower right to mask the distortion.
2. Three birds were liberated from their fabric and added to the quilt to give a more integrated feeling.

George has chosen to border his horizontal-row quilt. The left and top borders are from the same fabric but are cut in two widths. The remaining borders feature two fabrics, also cut in different widths. Notice how the trees extend into the right and left borders, which helps to soften the rigidity of the framing.

Above: *Sterne* (in progress)

Right: 16. *Sterne*. 46" x 49". George Taylor, Anchorage, Alaska, 1994.

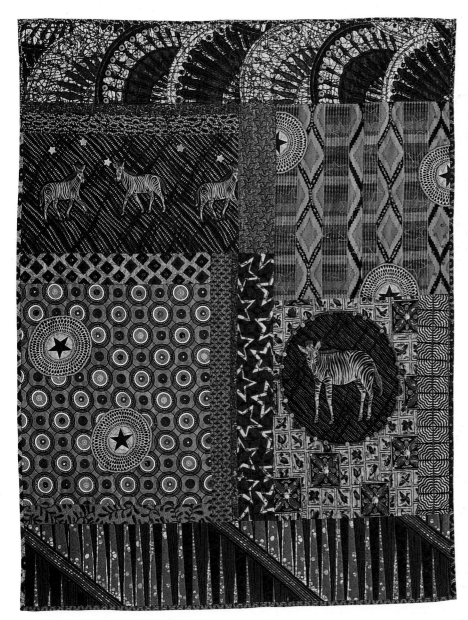

Opposite page: 17. *My Trip to Africa With Roberta.* 56" x 85". Stephanie Bennett-Strauss, Lafayette, California, 1994.

Left: 18. *Stars of Africa.* 42" x 54". Janet Shore, El Cerrito, California, 1993.

Above right: *Stars of Africa* Sections

Stephanie Bennett-Strauss has pieced a background of horizontal rows in *My Trip to Africa With Roberta.* The strips themselves have been vertically fragmented. Notice how effectively Stephanie has positioned the two light-green and the yellow strips. The diagonal beading helps to weave together all the rows. The borders do a nice job of pulling together the whole quilt. Notice the repetitions of fabrics and motifs in a staggered manner. Again, there is beading, this time in a zigzag pattern. All of these fabrics and embellishments are just the background for the magnificent women who saunter across the quilt. What fun to study their clothes and baskets.

SECTIONS

Making a quilt in sections is similar to working in rows, but the major seams don't go from top to bottom or side to side. One area is composed and then added to another. Eventually you work your way to the outside edges. Working in sections is not quite as neat and tidy as composing in rows. But it works!

Janet Shore worked with an assortment of gift fabrics to create *Stars of Africa.* She decided to make-do with the limited yardage. When Janet recognized that the zebra in the circle was her focus fabric, the quilt fell into place. The circle had to be liberated from its piece of fabric, which freed her to appliqué it onto another background. Notice that the zebra is not centered in the quilt like a bull's-eye.

The stars set into circles were also liberated. Three of these stars are fragmented because that's how the fabric had been cut. Following the seams, you can see that Janet's quilt is composed of four sections plus a top and bottom border.

Naomi Pockell began her quilt *The Road to Ouagadougou* as a composition built in rows. Her initial arrangement and her progress about midway when rows were still a feasible sewing method are shown here. When you study the right side of the finished quilt, you will see that Naomi had to switch to the sections format of assembly. Did you realize that Naomi has borders on only three of the edges of her quilt?

Joan Zott worked in sections on *It's A Jungle Out There!* She resorted to appliqué to attach the lower right-hand beige rectangle to the beige fabric above it. Appliqué will bail you out when piecing fails. The leopard is stepping gingerly over the resulting seam. Notice that Joan used this technique of having shapes extend over seams in several other places, which helps to soften the rigidity of the lines.

Above Left: *The Road to Ouagadougou* (in progress). Beginning Stage

Above Right: *The Road to Ouagadougou* (in progress). Midway

Right: 19. *The Road to Ouagadougou.* 64" x 75". Naomi Pockell, Lafayette, California, 1994. Finished Quilt

20. *It's A Jungle Out There!* 45" x 55".
Joan Vandercook Zott, Folsom,
California, 1994.

Composing of Quilt (Auditioning of Fabrics)

This book is about the joy of fabric! Let's get down to some concrete examples that illustrate how to use fabric in a more creative way.

VISUALIZING IN FABRIC

I love discovering the secrets printed on my fabric. Somewhere, I'm sure, is just the fabric I need for a particular look. Developing the necessary eye for such a job takes work but it's a fun part of the game named creativity.

First of all, you need the mind set, "I'm looking for ...." Having a focus allows you to narrow the possibilities as you peruse your fabrics. Hopefully you have some unusual and out-of-the ordinary candidates, not just small quilt prints (calicoes). The task might require a visit to a fabric store. I often buy fabric just because it's odd. I needn't know how I will ultimately use it when I purchase it.

The photo below shows two fabrics that I considered from my collection when I was making *Sangomas, Cocks, and Hens.* I instantly recognized their potential as rooster tails. Look at the drawing to the right which shows my free-hand cut pattern for the rooster in the upper left part of the quilt. Notice that the plume on the gold fabric isn't exactly, only approximately, like the pattern. Things don't have to be perfect—"good enough" will do. Left-brainers, stop being too literal. Remember, viewers of the quilt won't see your original pattern. They'll accept the image as you render it. This would be an example of what's commonly referred to as "artistic license."

The green/red fabric was used to produce the rooster in the lower

right part of the quilt. Below is the free-hand cut inspiration. Notice that once again the tail isn't identical to the pattern, which only served as a starting point. In order to have the tail point in the right direction, I had to use the wrong side of the fabric. As a bonus, I was also able to get the rooster's waddle from the rest of the red design. These examples of fabric visualization seem very obvious to me because I have already discovered them.

Left: African Fabrics in the Author's Collection

Above: Paper-cut Hen and Cock Patterns

Opposite page: 21. *Sangomas, Cocks, and Hens.* 61" x 81". Roberta Horton, Berkeley, California, 1992. Quilted by Janet Bales Dollard.

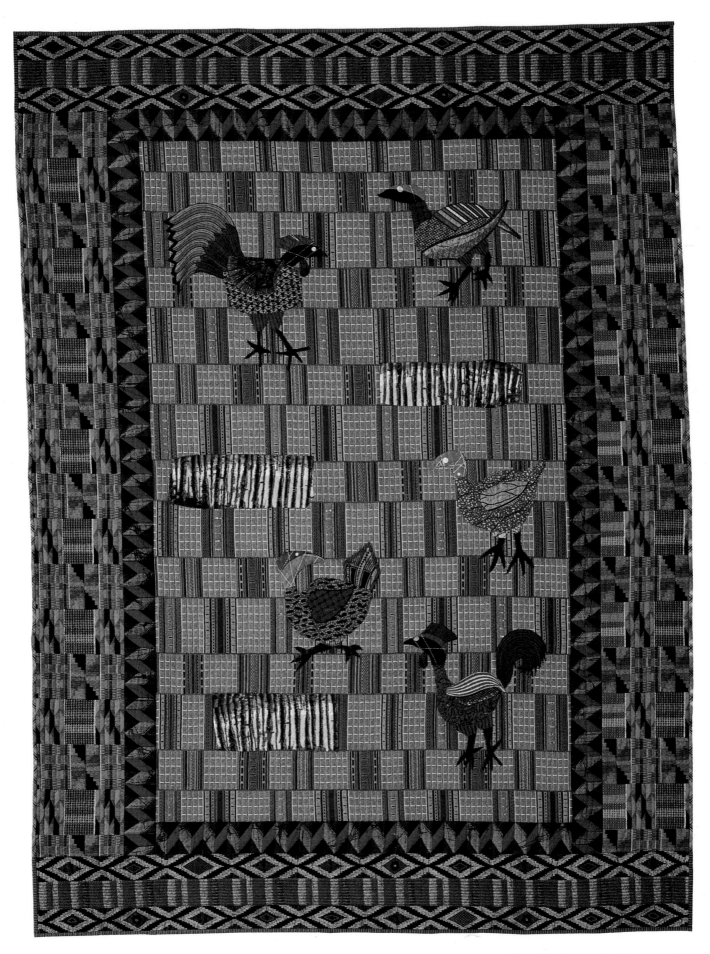

Study the photo of African fabric. Would you have thought "chicken" upon viewing this odd assortment? Stephanie Bennett-Strauss could, and did, when she made *My Trip to Africa with Roberta* (Quilt 17, page 44). Find the four fabrics in the resulting masterpiece shown above.

The trick to visualizing in fabric is to relax. Lay out your fabric so that you see a good representation of the design on each piece. As you scan these fabrics, you have to get beyond what the motifs are printed to be. You're not required to use an entire shape; sometimes you only need one section or area. Look for designs that approximate in size and shape what you need. If you're making a complicated shape, can it be broken down into individual parts? My rooster in the upper left part of Quilt 21 (page 49) used a total of six pieces of fabric to create the finished shape; the cock

in the lower right part used eight.

Let's look at a portrait gallery of people, which I consider the most difficult shape of all to render. The examples are each recognizable as humans but each rendition is different.

Christine Davis in *African Tapestry* (Quilt 15, page 42) created a simple pieced pattern to represent women. Because Christine free-form pieced (refer to Techniques: Piecing on page 88), there are slight irregularities between the people. None of us is the same as another individual, either. Three fabric choices were required per block: bandanna, dress, and background. What fun it must have been to select the women's wardrobes. Some of the females sport earrings, a necklace, a bracelet, or anklet.

Notice that the backgrounds Christine used are all different. The

Above: African Fabric Assortment

Above left: *My Trip to Africa With Roberta* (detail from Quilt 17). Stephanie Bennett-Strauss, Lafayette, California, 1994.

row is formed from the repeated blocks. It would have been easy to slip into the old habit of having the background uniform throughout. The fabric mixture makes the row of people better integrate into the mood of the rest of the quilt.

22. *African Impressions II: Sharing.*
44" x 48". Lorle Starling, Lake
Oswego, Oregon, 1994. Appliquéd
Women

Let's look at Lorle Starling's figures for *African Impressions II: Sharing.* She selected the same basic human shape as Christine Davis, except she chose to appliqué the heads, necks, garments, arms, and legs. The garments are really rectangles. Remember the design rule: **It's important that the line isn't straight.** The dresses were then decorated with smaller rectangles, neck rings, and chest adornments, which make the simple figures look much more complicated. All the shapes, including the vases, were free-hand cut (refer to Techniques: Appliqué on page 94.)

Also notice other ways in which Lorle used her fabrics in a creative way. The quilt is done in the horizontal row format. The background is made up of six strips of fabric, with the women spanning two of the rows. Working in this simple format allowed Lorle to effectively showcase her background fabrics. Four of the fabrics give the feeling of being composed from pieced units. Quilting on the design lines helped to emphasize this effect. The gray mosaic fabric was used on the wrong side (reverse side) to mute its pattern and value. Due to Lorle's selective choice of yardage, she got a lot for free—she was able to create much more than the limited number of original fabrics might suggest.

Only three of the fabrics in this quilt are actually from Africa. The printed diamonds in the second row are from Côte D'Ivoire. Some of the clothing and the unique hand-printed fabric across the bottom are from a small self-help project in South Africa. Yet all added together, Lorle was able to impart a flavor of Africa.

Facial details can be tricky. Did you notice that Christine Davis left the faces blank in her quilt (No. 15 on page 42)? Lorle Starling's faces were inspired by the Ndebele dolls shown here.

Jane Buys also used the shape of Ndebele dolls as the inspiration for her figure detail. She chose a great fabric to represent the blanket and wedding apron worn by Ndebele married women. The real apron is made from leather, which is then heavily adorned with intricate bead work. Jane used buttons on the apron area.

Masks are an easy way to create faces because you can resort to exaggeration. People don't have the expectation that masks will be realistic, which gives you more artistic license.

During an African Safari workshop, Joanne Baucum spied out of the corner of her eye a small warrior face image on someone else's piece of fabric. Suddenly her idea came together and she was ready to render her own interpretation of *Mask*. What looks like purple and yellow embroidery around the eyes and forming the nose is actually printed fabric. Joanne added the eyes and mouth. The eyebrows were printed; the forehead adornment was added. Eventually some wonderful beading was added to integrate all parts of the patchwork face.

The face image was very strong and needed something to counterbalance it, but at the same time, not detract from it. Once the eight diamonds were added, something was still not quite right. The free-hand cut zigzag across the bottom proved to be the needed unifying element. Many fabrics were auditioned before the right one was discovered. The composition is completed by a series of borders.

In the Face of Adventure is by Lynne Johnson. If you follow the vertical seamlines carefully you will see that they go from top to bottom, making this a vertical row quilt format. The masks are staggered to give a feeling of movement. The playful theme is enhanced by the uneven perimeter edge. The leaves are scattered throughout the composition, which helps to obscure the fact that the masks were appliquéd to rectangles. Rather than using a common pattern, each mask has a different personality. What a fun game it must have been to find all of the "proper" shapes for the eyes, noses, and mouths. Lynne worked with a mixture of machine and handwork and with all sorts of embellishments (refer to Techniques: Embellishments on page 105).

Above: Ndebele Dolls

Below: *Ndebele* (detail of Quilt 26, page 57). Jane M. Buys, Lynden, Washington, 1994. Ndebele Woman

Right: 23. *Mask.* 58" x 58".
Joanne Baucum, Walnut
Creek, California, 1994.

Below: 24. *In the Face of
Adventure.* 61" x 37". Lynne
Johnson, West Linn, Oregon,
1994.

PERSONALIZING FABRIC

When you buy fabric, the sales slip is a deed of ownership. But sometimes it doesn't feel like it's really yours, especially when someone else also uses it in a quilt. This particularly holds true for fabrics that feature a unique, highly recognizable motif. Therefore you must make your piece of fabric look somehow different from anyone else's. In other words, you must stamp yourself on it by personalizing it.

Look at the detail of a figure used by Joan Zott shown here. She has adorned it with a decorative bib cut from another fabric. Notice the diamond-pattern machine stitching across the body. The figure has been personalized.

Helen Streit has used figures from the same fabric in *African Magic*. Helen had such a good time playing paper dolls as she dressed her characters that by the time she was finished, she had completely layered over the original fabric cutouts! The upper right-hand doll cried out for a three-dimensional ruffled belt. The left-hand doll's dress is made from a Guatemalan fabric that was woven with dangling strings—they aren't an added embellishment. Helen also added buttons for the eyes.

Helen's people look great but her layering approach led to technical problems. Much to her disappointment, the area proved too thick to hand quilt. Perhaps Helen could have traced the body parts from the printed figures and used them as patterns. The birds on the right border are more modestly dressed, which prevented a build-up problem. Whenever possible, cut away any fabric that ends up underneath an appliqué shape. Remember to leave a proper seam allowance.

Above: *It's A Jungle Out There!* (detail of Quilt 20, page 47). Joan Vandercook Zott, Folsom, California, 1994. Personalizing a Fabric Image

Left: *African Magic* (detail of Quilt 14, page 41). Helen Streit, Davis, California, 1994.

LIBERATING ELEMENTS

When you work with a medium- or large-scale fabric that contains recognizable shapes, you may find it necessary to cut it up into the separate visual components to extend its usefulness. After all, it's yours; you already own it. It's okay to cut a hole out of it—you must get beyond that fear of cutting. In some cases, you may have been stymied as to how to effectively use the fabric as a continuous piece of yardage. In large-scale designs, it may be necessary to free the motif from the "busyness" around it so that you can better see and appreciate it. The remaining yardage may resemble Swiss cheese with all its holes.

Let's study *Almost African* by Nancy Candelo. Fan shapes free fall down the right edge of her quilt. The fan fabric is also used as continuous yardage strips in the upper left-hand and the lower right-hand free-form Log Cabin shapes. The bottom border fabric is used in the upper right-hand Log Cabin. It's fun to see both "cuts" of these two fabrics.

25. *Almost African.* 44" x 47".
Nancy Candelo, Davis, California, 1994.

Also notice the blue stripe Nancy appliquéd to the black strip. She decided to soften this line by fragmenting it toward the bottom. Just because it's printed as a continuous bar of color doesn't mean that you're obligated to use it that way!

By the way, originally the blue stripe was on the right-hand side of the black strip, which placed it dead center in the quilt. Two things were necessary to change the position: relocate the blue stripe to the left-hand side of the black strip and decrease the width of the left border. Both manipulations pushed the important blue line off center.

You also have the power to reconstruct a fabric to make it better suit your needs. You can add or take away elements. Joan Zott in *It's A Jungle Out There* (Quilt 20, page 47) worked with an unusual fabric shown here. Notice how she added a left-side black face to a right-side black face to create a whole face. The floating flowers above the keyholes were liberated from an all-over print and were used as separate units. Stephanie Bennett-Strauss also used this floral fabric to clothe the woman on the right in her quilt (Quilt 17, page 45).

INTEGRATING ELEMENTS

Motif fabrics can be used to integrate the quilt composition. Sometimes an area feels somehow different or out-of-kilter with the rest of the quilt. In *Ndebele* by Jane Buys, the upper section had a background that proved too light. A sun was added that partially extends into the border. The houses still looked like they were floating and needed to be grounded. The next step was the addition of some foliage. These remedial additions might be called "band-aids."

I call another integrating element "confetti." This refers to small shapes

Opposite page above: African fabric used in Quilt 20, page 47

Opposite page below; *Ndebele* (in progress). Quilt with the upper background section too light

Above: 26. *Ndebele.* 38" x 57". Jane M. Buys, Lynden, Washington, 1994. "Band-aids" added to integrate upper background area

such as circles or squares, which are usually floated across a surface. These light-hearted shapes are more of an embellishment, although they do important jobs like add or repeat a necessary color, move the eye, or fill up a void. Linda Atkinson used confetti in *My Sister's Lament* (Quilt 2, page 20).

(Quilt 2, page 20)

FABRIC BONUSES: THINGS WE GET FOR FREE

Take full advantage of all aspects of your fabric. Learn to approach it with an open mind and to really look at it with your eyes. We need to think in terms of opportunities presented to us.

Patching and Mending

I can remember my mother cutting bed sheets down the middle, then resewing the strips so that the selvage edges met down the center. This resulted in strong, under-used fabric in the middle and the worn fabric relocated to the outside edges. It was a frugal trick learned from her mother. The useful life of the sheet had been extended. Such thrifty practices have for the most part died out, and we have become a throw-away society. It seems easier to replace rather than repair.

What I'm saying extends beyond the textile world. All kinds of household items used to be repaired, sometimes in very ingenious ways. In earlier times, repairs were often made out of necessity because the goods themselves were scarce. Sometimes, there was a sentimental fondness for the item itself. During hard times there simply wasn't money available to replace worn items. And there was always the "waste-not, want-not" attitude. Any of these could be a reason for a repair.

A Collection of Mended Objects. Photo by Ben Blackwell. Courtesy of The Ames Gallery, Berkeley, California.

The photo here shows some examples of repair work. The teapot has a riveted copper replacement handle. The wooden bowl has tacked leather patches. The wooden spoon has a tin tip and patch. The copper pot has a replaced handle. The Shaker oval box has wire repairs in the lid. The crack in the porcelain platter is held together with eight staples. The apple basket has a big tin slat and a replaced bottom. Each repair is obvious because the patching element is different from the original material; no attempt has been made to hide it, perhaps because the items are utilitarian. Each repair results in an enhancement in the sense that the item is now unique; it's unlike any other of its kind. In a strange way, the repair is often beautiful.

Antique quilts often show evidence of patching, either to make a piece of fabric big enough to use or to repair some damage. Patching is part of the quiltmaking tradition. In fact, if you've been a quiltmaker long enough, you probably have had one or all of the following disastrous and/or frustrating experiences:

1. The fabric was accidentally cut wrong. You made an incision where you shouldn't have.
2. A slash was made into the fabric when you were trimming a quilting thread. The quilt top was all basted together and partially quilted.
3. Because of the way the design was drawn on the fabric, the whole motif couldn't be shown as you would have liked.

The first two cited examples are in the "whoops" category, and the third is a scenario revolving around the limitations of your fabric. Looking at these situations with your new creative outlook you should realize that all three represent patching opportunities. Let's study three of my quilts where I have dealt with patching.

In South Africa, I very much felt the need to make-do and recycle. Therefore, theme-wise, *Zebra Crossing* would be a perfect place for me to patch. The opportunity presented itself three times in the quilt. Some of my hand-dyed solids had come in a package that was filled with random-sized scraps. Two of the strips contained a fabric "marriage," that line of stitching sewn at the mill to join the end of one roll of fabric to the beginning of the next roll. Most

Zebra Crossing (detail). A Fabric Marriage

stores choose to cut out this section and not sell it, unless they place it on a remnant table at a discount. My "marriages" weren't stitched with the usual white thread because the fabric was hand-dyed. I was delighted with these treasures and included them in my free-hand cut Log Cabin blocks.

Notice the similarity between the "marriage" in my quilt block and the necessary stitching on the crack in the Shaker bowl shown below. Both patches are truly embellishments, which beautify the surface. Remember also that this is an example where "I got something for free."

Above: 27. *Zebra Crossing.* 46" x 35".
Roberta Horton, Berkeley, California, 1992.
Quilting by Janet Bales Dollard.

Right: Shaker bowl from the Alfred, Maine, community. Repaired by the colony cobbler, Joshua Bussell (as reported by sister Mildred Barker). Photo by Sharon Risedorph. Courtesy The Ames Gallery, Berkeley, California.

My next patching challenge involved the animal fabric I planned to use. Unfortunately, the artist rendered the animals in an overlapping fashion, which forced me to deal with the limitations of the fabric. Fortunately for me, there were spare zebra parts at the top and bottom edge of my ½ yard of fabric. I knew from the start that a perfect match would be impossible because the missing parts literally didn't exist.

Study the original American fabric and the *Zebra Crossing* detail of the resulting block made from that area. I was lucky that I had already chosen to do raw-edge appliqué because there wasn't fabric to spare for seam allowances. Look for my patches:

Left: American Fabric

Below: *Zebra Crossing* (detail of Quilt 27). Zebra made from American fabric

1. The stomach of the zebra was filled in to mask the giraffe's head.
2. A rear leg and tail had to be created where the elephant's trunk was in the way. The resulting legs were really too short but that was solved by placement on the background fabric. It looks like those legs are standing behind a rock.
3. The front leg needed a repair to mask out the elephant's ear.
4. A bush was added to cover the monkey's head and to help integrate the zebra into the background scene.

A third patching opportunity happened when I thought I was finished with the scene. It was pointed out to me that the dark areas I had considered rocks were really sea shells. I was crestfallen. Ultimately I added the rectangular beige patches that suggest dried grass. These are to divert your attention away from the "sea shell" rocks. Because they are a lighter value, it works since your eyes always go to white or light colors. I think they make the scene also look more realistic, so I came out ahead in the long run.

Now let's study another quilt, *Dutch Windows Lappendeken*. My strongest memory of a visit to the Netherlands is of the flower-filled, lace-curtained windows in the village houses. The lace-looking fabrics I selected for the bottom-right window had mysterious holes right in the area I wanted to use. There was no way to eliminate the three holes, so I patched by mending. I machine-stitched around each hole and then filled in the space with some stitches, sort of like darning a sock—a detail of a repair is shown on page 62.

Above: 28. *Dutch Windows Lappendeken.*
82" x 75". Roberta Horton, Berkeley,
California, 1994. Quilted by Janet Bales
Dollard

Right: A strong Dutch impression. (Photo
by Roberta Horton)

The butterfly on the vertical mullion in the lower right of the Quilt 28 is an example of patching to cover-up or to mask out something undesirable. If it were a pencil drawing, we could reach for an eraser. The blue mullions were topstitched onto the finished window composition rather than cutting the window into sections and piecing the blue strips into place. When I pressed with my iron, a ridge appeared on the blue fabric because of the satin stitching underneath it. Nothing would remove the mar, which I found distracting. The butterfly "band-aid" was added to obliterate the unsightly area. The patch was appliquéd after I had declared that the quilt was finished! Following the rule that "repetition makes things go together," I sewed more butterflies onto the quilt.

Above: Dutch Windows Lappendeken (detail). Repair Darning

Imperfections

Sometimes we elect to work with fabric that has already had one life—perhaps as a garment. The recycled fabric probably isn't in perfect condition, perhaps with stains, tears, holes, maybe even patches. The normal procedure would be to cut out the good parts and use them. Is this the only way to go?

I recently took a visiting quiltmaker to a show of quilts made from denim jeans. The britches quilts were wonderful and made you want to cut up a favorite old pair of pants. My guest confessed that she had made quilts from her husband's discarded work jeans for years. Because he is a sign painter, she had to carefully cut out the paint splotches and stains. Her comment was, "Oh, I left my husband out of the quilt!" Used fabrics can indeed add to the story.

Takayama Harajiku is a quilt I made from antique Japanese textiles that were either bought or given to me as gifts when I was in Japan. Made from mostly indigo dyes, the fabrics seemed to evoke for me the feeling of old Japan. Each time I share the finished quilt, memories seem to spring forward, some mine and some from a distant era.

The light blue fabric used for the sashing and part of the border was the single largest textile in my collection. The size of the fabric and the fact that it was unpatterned made it a perfect candidate for sashing. Upon

Opposite page: 29. Takayama Harajiku. 42" x 58". Roberta Horton, Berkeley, California, 1987.

Below: Takayama, Japan. (Photo by Roberta Horton)

spreading the piece out, I discovered that there was a bleached area spanning the width of the yardage. If I eliminated the fade, the strips would be too short. There was no way to ignore the light area so I decided to forge ahead. After all, hand-dyers of cloth are always discharging one color to add another. I got my special effect for free!

In the long run I think that my decision to use that particular fabric in its damaged state was to my advantage. The areas of discoloration allude to the antiquity of the textiles. Knowing what I do now, I regret that I didn't use sections of the printed fabrics that were also damaged. The holes would have required patches but I now know that is the fun part! Remember, a quilt merely shows what you knew when you made it. In 1986-1987, when *Takayama Harajiku* was made, I wasn't heavily into my "patching mode" yet.

A word of caution: Many antique textiles are too fragile to incorporate into our quilts. Always test for strength by gently pulling on them in both directions. At present, there are lots of reproduction fabrics, from both the 1930s and earlier periods, available in quilt stores. Their advantage is that they aren't delicate. More importantly, they give an automatic mind-set to the viewer.

The Selvage Edge

Some fabrics have an interesting selvage edge. I was fascinated by the elephants that marched across the selvage of some of my African fabrics. The selvage edge was wider and fortunately wasn't as thick or tightly woven as in most American fabrics. I found that if I pieced the edge into the quilt, I would lose ¼" of the design into the seam. My solution was to topstitch the fabric to the next one, thereby saving the whole exotic motif.

Look at the houses where Christine Davis included selvage edges in *African Tapestry* (Quilt 15, page 42). One door decoration includes the

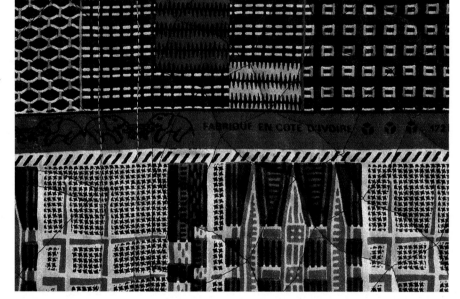

Ishmail's Revisited (backing of Quilt 12, page 38). Roberta Horton, Berkeley, California, 1992. A Beautiful Selvage Edge

country of origin. Another door frame sports color gams, those circles used to register rotary screens for the printing of the different colors.

Study the detail (page 62) of the lower right window of *Dutch Windows Lappendeken* (pictured on page 61). I had to include the selvage edge of my fabric in order to show the complete lace design for the curtain. This necessitated topstitching the selvage to the next fabric.

Auditioning, Selecting, and Attaching Borders

When considering borders for a quilt, most quiltmakers behave like they are making a visit to the local picture framing shop. One strip of wood or metal is selected to be used on all four edges. Of course, the corners will be mitered. We consider ourselves fancy if we add a mat. It would be even more daring to add a thin inner border or to have the interior edge of the mat painted another color.

Up-the-Ante Chart for Borders

Solid color
Small-scale print or plaid
Large-scale print or plaid
Same fabric all sides, uniform width
Same fabric all sides, varying widths
Different fabric on each side, uniform width
Different fabric on each side, varying widths
More than one fabric per side
Not all sides of the quilt have a border
Image from quilt interior intrudes into border
Width of border varies along one side

Quilts are another matter and afford us more choices. You're working with fabric, not wood and metal, so your corners don't have to be mitered unless the design of the quilt dictates it. You can use different fabrics, even different widths. If you have made a quilt that has the same fabric in a uniform width on all four edges, you have mastered that skill. Think about the possibilities listed in the chart here.

These are all options that you can choose. You may be able to think of some more. They are ranked from simple solutions to more challenging approaches. The first time that you create an adventuresome border may be scary. But they are very addicting, and you'll find yourself looking forward to bordering time.

Hope: A View From Broadway Terrace (page 66) is a quilt I didn't plan to make. There was a disastrous firestorm in the Berkeley-Oakland hills in October 1991. Three thousand homes were lost. I was away from home at the time and couldn't bring myself to view the area upon my return. I couldn't bear to go there until the following May. I was both saddened by the desolation and heartened by the sight of hillsides blanketed with golden poppies, the California state flower. These had been seeded by helicopters within days of the fire being extinguished in order to lessen the threat of erosion when it rained.

As soon as I got home, I had to go through my fabric collection, looking for meaningful fabrics to commemorate what I had just seen. The center of the quilt is a single half yard of fabric that I had forgotten buying. It reminded me of the aftermath of the fire: twisted steel, ashes, smoke. It said everything. I used it just as it had been cut, which was a slightly irregular rectangle.

California Poppies
(Photo by Roberta Horton)

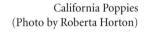

Hope: A View From Broadway Terrace . In progress

The detail on the previous page shows the quilt being composed. In this case, it was the borders that had to be composed. This is the only quilt I have ever made where the borders took longer to create and sew than the interior of the quilt. I free-hand cut pieces to audition them. These also weren't perfect rectangles. I got used to the resulting irregular edges and decided to leave them.

The finished quilt is No. 30. The black-and-white plaid helps to move your eye around the border. This fabric stands out because of the color white. I free-hand cut poppies from an abstract floral fabric that didn't actually contain poppies, so I was only able to make nine flowers. The poppies are meant to be the only color in the quilt, a welcome relief from all of the depressing black and gray.

Kente cloth is woven in Ghana in narrow strips. Multiple strips, sometimes of mixed patterns, are then sewn together to obtain the desired width of the textile. The real fabric is too heavy for quiltmaking. Fortunately, there are printed versions, which are perfect candidates for borders. The strips contain patterns that look like they are pieced—a good example of something for free. Keep an open mind when using *kente* cloth prints. There may be more than one way to cut the fabric (see below right).

George Taylor's *Trois Poissons* (Three Fish) uses three *kente* cloth prints. One has been used for the background. The right and bottom borders use two different strips from the second fabric. The third fabric appears on the left side. By the way, did you realize that the middle fish in the composition is from the same tree fabric that George used in his quilt *Sterne?* (See Quilt 16, page 43.) Look at the ground line, turn it vertically and mirror image it. What a versatile fabric!

30. *Hope: A View From Broadway Terrace.* 37" x 54". Roberta Horton, Berkeley, California, 1992. Quilted by Janet Bales Dollard and Roberta Horton.

Symmetrical Cut   Assymetrical Cut

Ways to cut the fabric

31. *Trois Poissons*. 48" x 46".
George Taylor, Anchorage, Alaska, 1994.

The inner-right and inner-lower borders are cut from one fabric. Dena Canty has used this same fabric for her left border in Quilt 10, page 36. Using a wider piece allows a folded illusion of depth to develop. Look at the basket in Tracy Allen's *Ester—A Tribal Star* (Quilt 9, page 34). This time, the fabric is used on the diagonal and reminds us of the woven patterns in a Zulu basket. Lynne Johnson embellished her piece of this fabric with Alder trimmings. Look for it in the lower left of *In the Face of Adventure* (Quilt 24, page 53). All of these quiltmakers have visualized in fabric.

Elaine Pruett has also chosen a fish theme in *At the Bottom of the Red Sea*. She elected to have her fish swimming in quilted water. The lower border feels more like the bottom of the sea as opposed to being a frame. Notice that several objects float over the top border. When Elaine quilted the top, right, and bottom borders, she ran stitching along the printed lines on the fabrics. This enhances the effect that the fabric is really pieced. So often the quilting inspiration is right there on the fabric—don't fight it. Don't be afraid of being too simple.

Lori Stephens in *Fishing With Roberta Under the African Sun* has allowed part of her story to take place in the border area. The hot sun and the clouds, some of which spout rain, are combined with a small moon, to give the weather conditions. The blue-and-yellow checkerboard at the top of the background area feels like sunlight reflecting from the surface of water. Lori has found some great fabric to compose her fish.

In *Celebrating Freedom*, Charlene Phinney originally had borders of about equal width on each edge, which proved to be quite static. At least the borders were of different fabrics. The quilt better captured the feeling of excitement when the rectangular panel was moved off-center by the addition of a *kente* cloth double strip to the right side—another application of the design rule: **"Don't center."**

Above: 32. *At the Bottom of the Red Sea.* 39" x 27". Elaine Pruett, Tehachapi, California, 1994.

Below: 33. *Fishing With Roberta Under the African Sun.* 49" x 60". Lori A. Stephens, Aloha, Oregon, 1994.

Opposite page: 34. *Celebrating Freedom.* 50" x 71". Charlene Phinney, Puyallup, Washington, 1994.

How do you decide which border fabrics to use? Once again, you must go through an auditioning process. I had decided on the fabric I wanted for the right and left borders of *Sangomas, Cocks, and Hens.* One of the photos here shows an arrangement in which the upper border seemed top heavy. The other shows what happened when I tried reversing the two borders. Now the quilt was bottom heavy. I ultimately decided to have the darker fabric used on both the top and bottom as shown in Quilt 21, page 49. Because those borders now were from the same fabric, I felt I needed to play some games to mess things up a bit. I added appliquéd diamonds in a random fashion. I also added beading to some of the diamond areas.

Zebra Crossing is shown here while it was being composed. As fate would have it, the finished shape wasn't a rectangle. The solution was to have a border that could accommodate the need for various widths of border fabrics. Therefore the border was sewn to units of the quilt, not to a finished quilt top. Because the border was going to be in segments, I had the opportunity to use various fabrics, which of course made the border ultimately more interesting.

My quilt top was feeling too dark. I had seen the savannah before the

Above left: *Sangomas, Cocks, and Hens* (Quilt 21 in progress). Roberta Horton, Berkeley, California, 1992. Upper Border Top Heavy

Above: *Sangomas, Cocks, and Hens* (Quilt 21 in progress). Lower Border Bottom Heavy

Below: A zebra crossing in South Africa. (Photo by Roberta Horton)

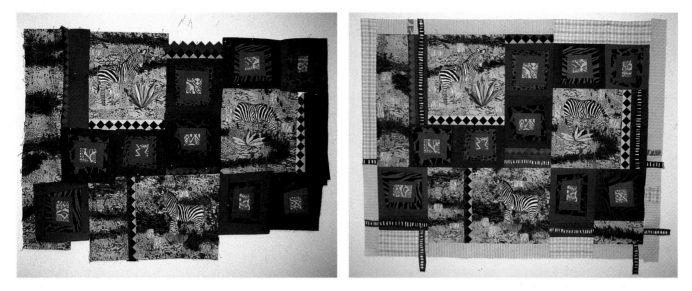

Above: *Zebra Crossing* (Quilt 27, page 59, in progress). Roberta Horton, Berkeley, California, 1992. Quilt Being Composed

Above Right: *Zebra Crossing* (Quilt 27 in progress). Border Auditioning

rainy season, so the grasses were tan and beige tones. Therefore, I chose light fabrics for the border area. I chose to work with stripes and plaids, which would just impart a feeling of texture and wouldn't detract from the interior of the quilt. Much to my surprise, the top became too light with the added border, so my next move was to add "band-aids." These related to lines that were already in the quilt. During the auditioning stage I tried more additions that you see in the finished quilt on page 59.

Borders are lots of fun to do if they aren't just the traditional same-fabric-on-all-four-sides variety. I have discussed other border solutions throughout the book as various quilts were shown. Borders are one more place that you can exercise your inventivity.

Composing the Backing

A popular rule for quilt backings is that they should be made from a fabric that is on the front of the quilt. Then you have merely to select from the already used possibilities. Remember that quilters always turn a quilt over, given the opportunity. A matching backing would be safe, but dull. The backing is another statement that you can make as a creative individual.

What happens if you go a step further? A more creative guideline would be that the backing should coordinate with the front, but be a surprise. This would eliminate fabrics already used on the front, because they represent no surprise. This opens up all kinds of possibilities that will require some more auditioning. I like to look at the front as I select the back.

Up-the-Ante Chart for Backings
Muslin or white
Fabric used on the front
Fabric that goes with the front, but is a surprise
Fabric that is a shock
Collage of fabrics
Pieced or appliquéd design

The front of *Takayama Harajiku* (Quilt 29, page 63) was made from serene antique Japanese textiles to evoke memories of the rural villages of old Japan. The back of the quilt, shown here, is made of contemporary fabrics I bought in Tokyo. Many pieces have English words printed on them, some misspelled. These fabrics reminded me of big-city Tokyo with all its noise, congestion, and advertising. Harajiku is a trendy district frequented by teens, which would epitomize these characteristics. When the quilt is turned over, it's a real shock to see the backing, but that's exactly what I wanted to happen—the jarring contrast between old and new.

Above left; *Takayama Harajiku* (back of Quilt 29). Roberta Horton, Berkeley, California, 1987. Contemporary Japanese fabrics used to compose a quilt back

Above: *Ishmail's Revisited* (back of Quilt 12). Roberta Horton, Berkeley, California, 1992. Printed *kente* cloths make the backing fabric collage look more complex.

Left: *Sangomas, Cocks, and Hens* (back of Quilt 21). Roberta Horton, Berkeley, California, 1992. A backing done in horizontal strips

Many of my quilt backings are made from several pieces of fabric. Since I usually buy half-yard pieces, it makes all my fabrics candidates for use on a backing. When I'm composing the backing, I pay attention to seam lines on the front. I don't want major seams on the front on top of major seams on the back. This is very important for hand quilting, where my goal is to keep everything as thin as possible. The seam positioning isn't as vital for machine quilting. In either case, I press open any backing seams to minimize layers.

Ishmail's Revisited (Quilt 12, page 38) has a collage of *kente* cloth prints for the backing shown here. This gives the feeling of intricate piecing. Five fabrics were used. The rod pocket across the top of the quilt was made from another strip.

Sangomas, Cocks, and Hens (Quilt 21, page 49) has a horizontal striped backing shown here. The black fabric was printed as a series of scenes. I cut the fabric apart, adding other strips to separate the vignettes. Twelve different fabrics were used. The huts are on a selvage edge, so that fabric was topstitched to the one above it. Can you see the rod pocket? I match my fabrics when I have sufficient fabric.

Up-the-Ante Chart for Bindings

Solid color
Small print
Stripe or plaid
Big print
All edges the same
Not all edges the same
Pieced along edge itself
Edge not a straight line

Selecting and Attaching Bindings

Quilt bindings are important because they're usually the final statement you make on a quilt. Sometimes the binding should not be noticeable to just blend into the border. At other times, the quilt needs a finishing accent or some spots of color. Think about this: People always touch the binding as they handle your quilt.

My normal procedure in selecting a binding is to pull several candidates from my fabric collection and try each one. The quilt top is pinned to my design wall. This permits me to insert the candidates behind the top, allowing just the finished binding edge amount to protrude. They can be pinned back over the border edge to look even more realistic. I need to judge the result up close as well as in a position standing back from the quilt. Through comparison, I can then determine which fabric does the best job.

When I made *Zebra Crossing* (Quilt 27, page 59), I ended with a light border to suggest the openness of the African plains. I decided that my binding should also be light to continue this mood. My left-brain had done a critique and come up with that guide line. Now I had only to look through the beige fabrics piled in my cupboard. I had no idea what my choice would be as I went through the assortment. This time, my eyes spied a small-scale fabric that featured African animals. I had owned it so long that I had forgotten it. I went no farther. It felt right! I went with my intuition.

Zebra Crossing (detail of Quilt 27). Roberta Horton, Berkeley, California, 1992. Appropriate Binding Fabric

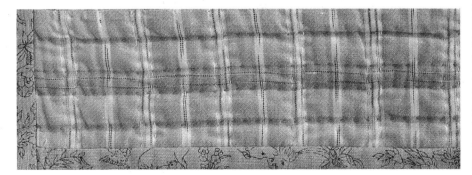

Care needs to be taken when you bind a quilt. The goal is to have a quilt that lies flat or hangs well, without rippling. Most quilts end up bigger around the outside edges than they are across the middle. The edges stretch as you handle them. If you're not careful, you can compound this problem when you sew on the binding. If you merely cut binding and pin it onto the quilt, you may in fact be adding to the perimeter width or length.

The binding needs to be measured as described here. A correctly measured binding can shrink in some of the fullness. Bias bindings stretch more than those cut on the straight grain so they are appropriate for curved edges. I make straight edges; therefore I most often use straight grain bindings.

When I'm working with plaids or stripes, I sometimes prefer the look of diagonal lines. I try the directional fabric both ways. I use on grain if I need the binding to be calm; I use bias if I want movement or agitation.

If it's necessary to splice a binding, I prefer to make a seam that's perpendicular to the edge because that's the easiest way. The exception would be if the border contains diagonal lines. Such was the case in *Dutch Windows Lappendeken* (Quilt 28, page 61), which had triangles in the border.

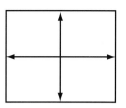

Measure Width and Length.

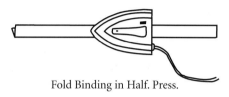

Fold Binding in Half. Press.

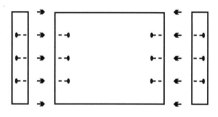

Attach Exact Measurement Bindings.

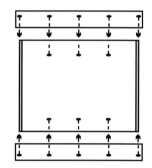

Attach Bindings With Added Seam Allowance.

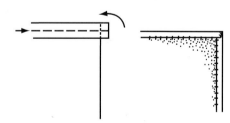

Turn Binding and Stitch.

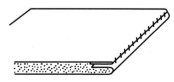

Alternate Method: Whip Stitch Front to Back.

Procedure for Binding A Quilt:

1. Measure across the middle of quilt in both directions to determine width and length. The edges may have stretched so don't measure these.
2. Cut binding fabric 2" wide. Fold strips in half lengthwise; press in an up-and-down motion. Ironing with the back-and-forth method will stretch the fabric.
3. Lay binding strips on table or floor. Measure and cut two opposite sides the exact measurements from Step 1. Add ½" seam allowance to the measurement for the other two sides and cut.
4. Pin the two exact-measurement strips to two opposite sides of the quilt on the front side, right sides and raw edges together. I find it helpful to mark both the quilt and the binding at ¼, ½, and ¾ points and then to match together at these spots. Ease the quilt top if necessary as you pin. Stitch through all layers. Turn to back, pin, and hand stitch.
5. Attach binding to the two remaining sides following the directions in Step 4. Remember not to count the ¼" seam allowance at each end when you divide the strip into fourths. Match binding to quilt top at corresponding points, remembering to extend ¼" seam allowance at each end. Pin and sew. When you hand stitch the back, you will need to turn in the seam allowance at both ends and overcast the ends.

Sometimes you won't want to confine your fabric in a square or rectangular shape. If a quilt has an irregular edge, you may find it too difficult to use a traditional binding. In that case, you will need to whip-stitch the front and back together as shown here. The bottom edge of Diane Goff's *Autumn Wind* (Quilt 38, page 80) was resolved in this manner.

Above; *Avis Africanus* (detail of Quilt 4).
Judy Hopkins, Anchorage, Alaska, 1993.
Information written directly on quilt with
permanent marking pen

Right: *Zebra* (detail of Quilt 11). Sylvia
Pressacco. Menlo Park, California, 1994.
Africa-Shaped Label

Below: *Dutch Windows Lappendeken*
(detail of Quilt 28). Roberta Horton,
Berkeley, California, 1994. Bernina sewing
machine generated label adorned with
Japanese *yukata* fabric

Labeling the Quilt

Quilts should have an identifying label on the back. Here is the information you might want to include:
1. Quilt's title
2. Your name
3. Your town and state (include country if quilt will travel)
4. Year made
5. Measurements
6. Name of quilter, if different than maker
7. Other applicable information such as a story about the quilt, special fabrics used, or gift to an individual

Various methods can be used to get the information on the label:
- Permanent marking pen
- Sewing machine writing
- Typewriter or computer printer

Judy Hopkins (Quilt 4, page 23) used the easiest solution and wrote directly on her quilt back. This would be risky if you tend to be messy or happen to misspell words easily. But then—you can always make a second label to patch over the mistake!

Labels don't have to be square or rectangular. Sylvia Pressacco (Quilt 11, page 37) used the outline of Africa for her label. The printing and sketch were done with a permanent marking pen.

Many sewing machines will write. Some even feature a memory that allows you to save and regurgitate vital statistics like your name and address to use over and over again. See the label for my *Dutch Windows Lappendeken* (Quilt 28, page 61).

Writing the information with a computer printer allows you to easily say more. You can also use your spell check device. I'm not a skilled enough typist to use a typewriter directly onto fabric, where the first effort counts.

◉ I have long been fascinated with the beauty and diversity of Japanese textiles. I live in the San Francisco Bay area where these fabrics have always been available, both visually and for purchasing. After all, I'm repeatedly told by the media that I live on the Pacific Rim. Today, many of our American fabrics are also very Japanesque in design.

Originally I elected to work in Japanese *yukata* cloth, which is used for cotton summer kimonos. Early on in my quiltmaking career, I made the decision that I'm a cotton person—that it's my fabric of choice. I considered the regal silks used in more elegant kimonos very beautiful but I personally found that silk was too slippery for composing directly on the design wall (pins had to be used to secure the pieces, and these were distracting to my left brain). Silk is often bonded to a fusible to make it more manageable in the sewing process, but I found that I disliked the resulting stiffness.

Well, my silk dilemma was eventually resolved because the designs usually reserved for silk began to be printed on cotton fabrics. Now I could engage my curiosity and see what happened when I tried this different flavor of textiles. The fabrics are colorful and busy, often large scale. Where to cut? That same old question.

While exploring this new territory, I decided to study more about Japanese design. Restrictions are always helpful in that they force you to work within new limitations, not just the same old comfortable way. I came up with a new formula, more guideposts to follow in my efforts to find different ways to work. Here are some of the options or possibilities to consider:

1. Asymmetry rather than being symmetrical
2. A diagonal axis rather than a centered medallion approach
3. A collage background composed of checkerboards or random-sized pieces
4. Patching or overlay of one design over another
5. Strive for irregularity of design rather than reward sameness of repetition
6. Areas of composition that fade away so not all the surface is equally important visually
7. Play on the contrast of geometric and floral designs

I found that these new design ideas could be used with the basic concepts and work processes that I have been advocating in the rest of this book. I include the following quilts as an example of working with a different kind of fabric, which caused new things to happen. The fabric once again makes the quilt....

35. *Bamboo Grove.* 36" x 69". Helen Temple
Cummins, Carmichael, California, 1994.

⚫ Helen Temple Cummins says that the design process for *Bamboo Grove* was "an intriguing one for me because normally I am the eternal planner. We [students] were forced to allow an evolution from a central theme or fabric into a finished piece. After immersing ourselves in the fabrics, the designs, and the culture they are a product of, we began. For me, this process was alive from start to finish—always subject to change—always calling on me to look again...."

The bamboo fabric was Helen's starting place. Notice how the quilting and sashiko stitching are an extension of the pattern beyond the physical edge of that fabric. The red sashiko across the bottom mimics design elements already used. The plum blossoms are borrowed from the upper right; the stair-step pattern continues from the *ikat* fabric above. The hemp leaf design is the same as that used in the borders. On purpose, Helen selected a thin batting to make the *sashiko* quilting—done with a heavy thread—easier to do.

Picking up a book on Japan, Helen discovered that the size of the *tatami* mat is twice as long as it is wide. She was amazed that her quilt had closely approximated those dimensions.

Helen was able to display a wonderful assortment of Japanese fabrics. To those she added several plaids and stripes in the interior and a stripe for the binding. By the way, the calligraphy done on the Japanese indigo fabric in the upper left-hand corner stands appropriately for "temple."

⬡ Tish Chung had the following comments about her *Japanese Garden on a Foggy Day:* "Learning to create a quilt with the philosophy of 'letting the fabrics design the quilt' was a new and difficult concept to understand, adopt, and absorb at first. I was reluctant to let go of my traditional, more comfortable, and predictable ideas concerning color, fabric, and design in relation to quiltmaking.

"…to begin a project without any preconceived ideas of the end result forced me to learn to feel free to play again, just as a child does. I stretched and pushed and pulled, changing and rearranging, until something of a quilt began to emerge from what was once a chaotic pile of unrelated textiles. Then it was as if the light came on, and I saw with brand new eyes. This experience was both a most challenging one and also a most freeing one."

Four different blue fabrics are used for the borders. If you think about it, each features an inner border, but none of the borders is executed in a purely traditional way. The top and bottom borders, using two different fabrics, are of equal width and are intersected by a matching 1" red strip. The right-hand border has a traditional 1½" printed strip for the inner border, but the color doesn't match any of the other inner borders. The left-hand border is much harder to describe, let alone decide how much of it is inner border and how much of it is part of the interior background. The narrow pink insertion is a folded pleat rather than the expected pieced strip. The flowers float over this division, helping to mask the boundaries. Tish certainly went beyond the standard border approach of using the same fabric in the same width on all sides.

Tish used metallic thread for the raw edge appliqué of the floral

clusters and butterflies. She machine topstitched the calligraphy strips with matching thread. The subtle blue-stripe background fabric was enriched by using metallic thread for the hand quilting. An ecru cotton quilting thread was used for the rest of the quilting, providing a nice contrast between shiny and dull.

36. *Japanese Garden on a Foggy Day.* 39" x 55". Letitia Chung, San Francisco, California, 1994.

37. *Serenity.* 50" x 50". Roberta Horton, Berkeley, California, 1993. Quilted by Janet Bales Dollard and Roberta Horton.

⊛ In my *Serenity* quilt, I decided to work with the diagonal axis idea. Notice that the background of my quilt is composed of the same design printed in two color ways. A *shibori*-like print slices through the piece, providing a contrast between geometric and floral.

Prior to composing the quilt, I had been studying a book on antique Japanese kimonos. I was fascinated to discover that some of the kimonos were made with recycled fabrics to extend the life of a precious textile. There were examples of patching. One fascinating piece of yardage was even woven to look like it was a collage of fabric pieces that overlapped each other.

Being inspired, I decided to try some overlay patching. I found another fabric that had similarities in flower construction to my background. I didn't use one design in two color ways as that would have been too simple a solution. I wanted the resulting image to be "not quite right." The patching fabric happened to be printed in a peculiar brick format that featured individual diagonal rectangles of design. I had never known how to use this fabric. With my new focus, it became the obvious choice for my patches. I was able to cut five from my standard half-yard piece of fabric.

The patches were hand appliquéd to the background with a hidden stitch. I wanted to accent the patches so I also sewed *sashiko* thread in a large running stitch as a decoration around the perimeter of each patch. You can say that I made this quilt so that I could have the opportunity to patch.

The right and left border fabric suggested a simple diagonal grid quilting pattern. Rather than getting caught up in the complexity of trying to quilt around the fan shapes in the top and bottom border fabric, I opted for an all-over fan design. The interior area is heavily quilted in matching threads to provide a beautiful texture. The exception is in the solid black and blue background areas where contrasting metallic thread is stitched in flowing lines. Here the stitches have a chance to be seen.

By the way, five butterflies skim across the surface of the quilt to add to the feeling of serenity. Can you find all of them?

38. *Autumn Wind.* 52" x 40". Diane Goff, Oakland, California, 1994.

Opposite page: 39. *The Other Side of Air.* 52" x 44". Michaele Call, Orinda, California, 1994.

⊛ Diane Goff's composition, which she calls *Autumn Wind,* is also divided by a diagonal axis. Leaves sail down this line—right off the edge of the quilt. Part of the background is built from a checkerboard. Note how the value changes and how some of the squares have broken free.

Borders appear only on the right and left sides. The right border blends more into the body of the quilt because of the similarity of values along that edge. The left-hand border appears stronger because there's a higher value contrast along that line.

Notice how the normal division between the left border and the background is obscured by the continuation of one fan shape into the background. Rectangles of fan sticks also float like debris from a whirlwind. Some circles from the right-hand gold fabric have even migrated over to the gray fabric. All of these additions helped to integrate the quilt. Remember the rule about repetition making things go together? In this situation the motifs were found on fabrics that were already in use elsewhere in the quilt. Diane comments, "I like the concept 'The fabric makes the quilt.' It's true in my case.... they are my inspiration."

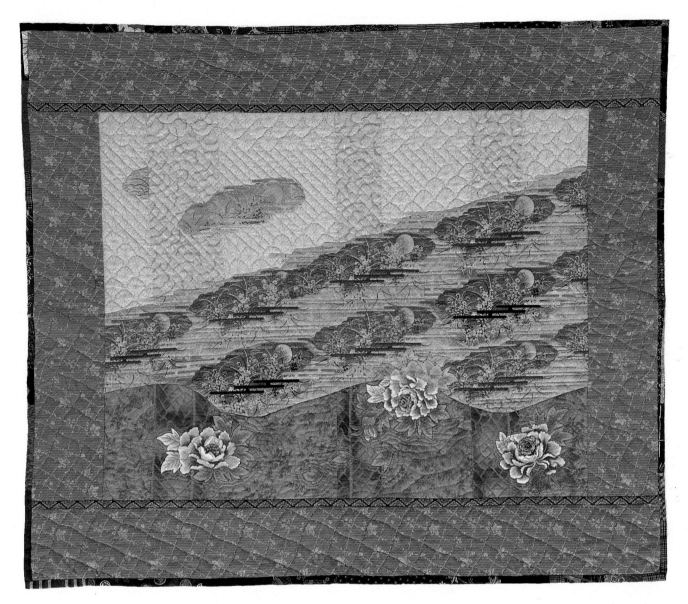

⊛ Mike Call said about *The Other Side of Air:* "This was the hardest project that I've ever attempted—from designing the quilt top to the last quilting stitch. My stated goal was to have a restful, peaceful quilt that reflected the simplicity and asymmetry of Japanese design. I kept fighting this concept by wanting to complicate the design. I also wanted to include all my vast mixture of Japanese fabrics. The conflict was resolved when I decided to use only a few important fabrics on the front; many of the remaining fabrics are on the back of the quilt.

"One of the gifts or surprises that occurred while making the quilt happened when I put the quilt together. I brought the edges of the back around to the front during the quilting stage and found the *yukata* cloth mixed with other American and Japanese fabrics made a wonderful binding for the front.

"I tried to not restrict myself regarding techniques and to think in terms of the finished results. I did both hand and machine appliqué, adding many pieces to my base fabrics. I painted on fabric with Versatex textile paint to achieve a translucent mist effect. I even created a three-dimensional look for the flowers.

"The quilting patterns were another fight. I tried complicated designs but found that I needed to maintain the integrity of the quilt by quilting patterns that reflected the simplicity of the design and the fabric of the quilt. Therefore, in the borders and upper third of the quilt, the stitching merely repeats lines present on the fabrics. The flowers in the flowing water needed a softer echo quilting design.

"Often I had to wait for the fabric to tell me what quilting design to use. Thus many hours were spent studying the fabric and design until the answer came. I think that I really grew as the quilt evolved—especially in listening to the quilt—patience, silence, simplicity. I feel the quilt will be a restful focus for reflection and meditation."

◉ Nadi Lane had this to say about the design process for her *Genso No Sekai:* "The class was wonderful but the time constraints made it very intense. When I took the pressure off by allowing myself not to resolve the project in class, the solution happened. The very next morning I awoke with the idea of depicting a landscape. The mountain at the lower right provides something for the clouds of flowers to hover around. The bottom border is pieced to simulate a lake and lake shore where the lone flower has fallen from an unseen cloud. When I got out of the way...the fabric dictated!"

The English translation of the title of this quilt is "World of Fantasy." Nadi has used a fabric for her background that gives the illusion of shadows or mists. To soften the horizontal lines on the fabric, notice that she added five same-fabric patches, which skim across the surface at varying angles.

Though appliqué is not Nadi's favorite technique, she felt it was a necessary evil. The flowers are hand appliquéd. Notice that a few small flowers have broken away from the big clusters. The hillside is raw-edge appliqué. Free-hand machine embroidery with a rayon thread has been added along this edge. The project is then elegantly hand quilted.

40. *Genso No Sekai*. 55" x 46". Nadi Lane, Agoura, California, 1994.

41. *Autumn Peonies.* 58" x 46". Sue Pruyn, Oakland, California, 1994.

✺ Look at the reds and pinks used by Sue Pruyn in *Autumn Peonies*. The background is a red-orange. The upper inner border is a dark pink (red with a blue tone). Now combine these two reds with the variety of reds found in the peonies. While auditioning yardage, the answer might be no. In the quilt, the answer is yes. Did you notice that there are both yellow-greens (the vertical strip) and blue-greens (the diamonds)? The choice of the reds and the greens are a good example of purposely mismatching colors. The vitality of the quilt comes from this startling color usage.

Look at Sue's borders. She has chosen a gold metallic finish fabric to use on all four sides. The fabric has the richness of an *obi*. You will notice, however, that the inner borders aren't identical, with the top one both a different color and width. A peony and diamond break into the bottom border.

Sue had this to say: "In designing the quilt, the overwhelming feeling I had was of freedom. At one time I studied painting, both oil and Oriental styles. My feeling in the quilt design process was similar to what I felt in using paints—being able to let myself go and to experiment and to find what 'felt' right.

"The idea of trying raw-edge appliqué was very challenging to me, but it seemed to suit the fabric perfectly, so I used it despite my innate aversion to that which I would normally consider unfinished looking. Now I'm glad I used the technique."

⊛ Nancy Bardach says that working with original kimono-patterned fabrics in her *Mountain Blossoms Pursue the Rising Sun* was a good, solid way to focus her thoughts on the spirit of Japanese design. Initially I had class participants do some free-hand cutting and sewing of a random gift assortment of Japanese textiles. She says, "This exercise helped me to loosen up my images and to cut bravely." Thus emboldened, Nancy cut into a fabric that suggested to her geometric slabs of color and had a strong, heavy appearance. With some patching, a volcanic mountainscape emerged.

The composition then needed a serene background, which was composed of squares and rectangles. She says, "This collage approach gave me more flexibility in adding a color where I wanted it. I could exaggerate the sense of movement, such as wind blowing the blossoms. The combination of rough edges and textured silks in an orderly array were, for me, the Japanese influence of irregularity on this design."

Nancy continues, "Raw-edge appliqué seemed very appropriate for the pink flowers. It gave them more lightness and delicacy. Their edges seem more lacy and vulnerable, similar to real flowers. The technique also allowed me to leave a ⅛" border of the light blue background around the clusters. This was helpful in bringing the flowers out more strongly against the muted colors of the background area.

"Moving the florets around was fun. I could see that the more exciting arrangements were those with a sense of movement to suggest the wind blowing. I exaggerated this feeling, which in turn inspired me to include the idea of wind when I created the title of the quilt."

Nancy chose to work with a polyester batt, which requires minimum quilting. The sparse amount of quilting gives the piece the soft puffy look of a silk futon. Notice that the solid fabric areas in the background allowed the quilted swirls to show to best advantage.

42. *Mountain Blossoms Pursue the Rising Sun.* 55" x 73". Nancy Bardach, Berkeley, California, 1994.

◉ Sally Ann Davey found each phase of making *Midnight Tide Pools* to be enjoyable. The design portion fell into place as soon as she followed the suggestion of starting with her favorite fabric, a panel that contained the *geisha*. Once the figure was liberated from her white background, she could be inserted onto a wonderful collage of dark fabrics that Sally created (a new idea for her). Notice that the four units that comprise the background aren't equal in size. Another new idea. She said, "It was fun to combine piecing and appliqué to create a feeling rather than a pattern."

Sally remembers me suggesting, "When you want to create Japanese, think asymmetrically." She says, "Being asymmetrical appealed to my rebellious nature. New ideas for me were that all the borders didn't have to be the same and that the sashing could extend into the border. Even the red screen pattern didn't have to be centered in a section."

The new open approach for Sally continued right on into the quilting stage. The quilting pattern could be changed within the composition rather than staying uniform throughout. Seamlines could be ignored, with patterns traveling over the natural divisions. It was also possible to use a variety of threads when quilting to create different feelings. Sally used quilting, *sashiko*, and metallic threads. Midway through composing the quilt, she discovered the poem shown in the photo here, which she sewed to the back of the quilt.

Above left: 43. *Midnight Tide Pools*. 39" x 56". Sally Ann Davey, Orinda, California, 1994.

Left: Izumi Shikibu, *The Ink Dark Moon*, New York: Random House, 1988.

"To A Man Who Used To Visit Secretly But Asked To Come Now In Day light"

There are many
Strange and lovely things
That swim in the midnight tide pools ....
I think I do not want to share them
With other divers' eyes by day.

44. *Sengen.* 42" x 41". Barbara Stone,
Albany, California, 1994.

⊛ Barbara Stone says of *Sengen,* "My original goal was to combine two disparate fabrics in one harmonious piece. I wanted the composition to incorporate as much of the Japanese aesthetic viewpoint as possible: diagonals, asymmetry, and checkerboards. I wanted to experiment with color combinations that are non-Western so I started with an orange fabric covered with flowers, streams, and *sashiko* patterns. As an anchor for my left-brain mentality, I added the three floating world figures.

"Initially, it seemed that the concreteness of the figures would help design the quilt. Instead, it added an 'edge' that isn't an element of Japanese quiltmaking. Figurative representation is antithetical to the understated, softly spoken approach of Japanese culture.

"But I wanted to use the courtesans. Finding a Japanese poem by Hiroshige enabled me to compromise. The orange fabric became Spring with streams filled with peach blossoms; the courtesans became Taoist immortals. Clouds were added around the figures not only to represent Heaven *(Sengen),* but also to mask out the other figures on the piece of yardage. The immortals aren't centered on the piece but hover as part of both the landscape world and the sky world. They are essential without being integral."

The cool blue-and-green checkerboard border was added to reduce the percentage of orange in the quilt. Notice that the upper background area is composed of two different fabrics, which are intersected with two contrasting panels.

"Swallows and Peach Blossoms Under a Full Moon," *Hiroshige, Birds & Flowers,* New York: George Braziller, Inc., in association with The Rhode Island School of Design, 1988.

We all have established techniques and methods that we follow as we sew a quilt together. But the sewing process itself can be just as exciting as the designing and fabric selection processes that have been discussed. We need to continue to stretch and grow even in the assembly stage of quiltmaking. Let me share some ideas with you....

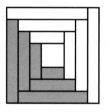

Traditional Log Cabin

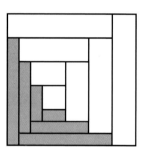

Off-Center Log Cabin

Piecing

As an American quiltmaker I usually think of piecing and templates and graph paper all in conjunction with each other—sort of "joined at the hip." At some point in my quilting career, I realized I could free-form piece. My patch-work could change and evolve just as my appliqué does.

The easiest way to understand free-form piecing is to make a free-hand cut Log Cabin block. By the way, this is a good way to begin to understand how your fabrics work together when they're sewn. It's a non-threatening way to start on your quilt especially when you're working with fabrics that are radically new to you. You can check on pattern similarity, value relationships, etc. The block doesn't even have to be used or it may be worked into the composition for the backing.

Traditional Log Cabin blocks are made with a square center and logs that are cut a consistent width throughout. An off-center Log Cabin is also made with a square center. The logs on the light side match each other in width; the logs on the dark side match each other in width, but differ from the measurement of the light side.

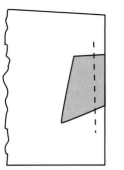

Step 1. Sew center to fabric #1 (right sides together)

Free-hand cut Log Cabin blocks don't have to start with a square center. Each log is cut separately, and the strips aren't parallel. What fun! Here is the procedure:

1. Place center shape on straight edge of fabric #1, right sides together. Sew. Press seam allowance towards fabric #1.

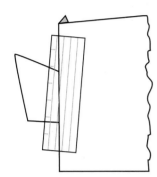

Step 2. Determine cutting angle

2. Position construction right side up on cutting mat. Place ruler on top, initially parallel to the joining seam. Move the ruler back and forth until you find an interesting angle. Don't forget that you will need the standard ¼" seam allowance, and make sure you allow enough fabric to show.

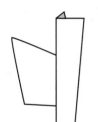

Step 3. Cut unit off of fabric #1

3. Cut the strip longer than you need. You mainly want to free the construction from fabric #1.

Step 4. Trim

4. Trim excess length off strip, using edges of center shape as a guideline.

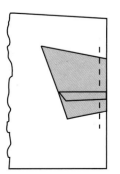

Step 5. Sew to fabric #2. Repeat Steps 1-5

5. Lay construction on fabric #2, right sides together. Repeat Steps 1-4.
6. Continue the process until the block is either big enough or the composition feels completed. As you build on additional strips, remind yourself that you may eventually want a shape that's sort of square. If you need a true square, make the last four strips wider than necessary. This will give you enough fabric to true-up the block into a square.

Joan Helm began *Jambo Africa!* with the construction of four free-hand cut Log Cabins. She allowed their arbitrarily finished shapes to determine what happened next in her quilt. Coping wedges were added to make the rows uniformly wide. Sashing was added to make the rows long enough. The free-hand cut Log Cabin blocks were pieced into the quilt. If you really study the quilt, you will see that it looks visually much more erratic than it really is.

45. *Jambo Africa!* 44" x 47". Joan Capron Helm, Portland, Oregon, 1992.

In *African Critters,* by Susan Maynard Arnold, the free-hand cut Log Cabins are also irregular in shape. The blocks have been appliquéd onto the *kente* cloth print, giving the appearance that they float across the surface. By the way, Sue is a confirmed piecer, and I was elated to finally get her to do some appliqué, using the raw-edge method.

46. *African Critters.* 51" x 60". Susan Maynard Arnold, Albany, California, 1994.

Above: *Walkabout* (detail of Quilt 6).
Roberta Horton, Berkeley, California,
1991. Two Log Cabin blocks

Opposite page: 47. *Almost African.*
49" x 62". Louise Colbert, Anchorage,
Alaska, 1993

Louise Colbert has both pieced and appliquéd her Log Cabin blocks into *Almost African*. Notice the two partial people blocks that seem to peek out from another layer. The color yellow moves your eyes through the quilt. The sun shapes and fish are liberated motifs from other fabrics.

When I was making *Walkabout* (Quilt 6, page 29), I wanted to use an Australian fabric that featured people. The fabric design prevented me from cutting a tidy square around each person. If I had done that, I would have cut off another character's hand or foot, rendering that figure unusable for another block. My goal was to use as many of the little men as possible in my precious half-yard of fabric. Study the photo here. My task was to add triangular inserts of solid fabrics that would bring my shapes out to straight lines so that I could add on my free-hand cut logs. If you think about it, the people are the center units for the Log Cabin blocks. This truly was free-hand piecing at its most exciting!

Appliqué

What is appliqué? Simply put, it's a method of attaching or sewing one shape to another. Look at Joan Zott's sun shape. This isn't appliqué as most traditional quilters would execute it. But, is the sun attached in a permanent way to the background? I think so; there's no danger of it falling off the quilt. Yes, we can extend the period of creativity right into the sewing stage.

No Cuervo by Judy Hopkins is another example of unconventional appliqué. Judy added a mola-like "outline" to her shape to provide more contrast with the background. Rather than doing reverse appliqué by hand, she simply inserted two additional fabric layers between the snake and the background. All layers of the snake were attached with raw-edge appliqué. Would you have guessed that the black-and-white outline is created by a black-and-white checkerboard fabric?

Machine Appliqué

One of the reasons that I made *Dutch Windows Lappendeken* (Quilt 28, page 61) was so that I could experiment with the new threads and bonding agents now available. The photo here shows one of the blocks where I was playing with some of these threads. The bouquet and flower pot were first sewn down with a small straight stitch. To the flowers I next added a small zigzag stitch done with a Sulky® rayon variegated thread. On the flower pot, I purposely varied the width of the zigzag stitch and used a metallic for some of the added straight stitching. A satin stitch was used for the blue saucer.

Raw-edge appliqué is a perfect technique for those of you who don't like to appliqué. A tiny straight machine stitch is taken around the perimeter of the shape. Depending both on the fabric and the amount of raveling you want, the line of stitching would be placed anywhere from $\frac{1}{16}$" to $\frac{1}{4}$" from the edge. I recommend stitching around the shape twice. The second row of stitching doesn't have to perfectly line up with the first. In fact, the second time around might be stitched in another color. The appliqué in *Zebra Crossing* (Quilt 27, page 59) was sewn in this manner.

It's a Jungle Out There! (detail of Quilt 20, page 47). Joan Vandercook Zott, Folsom, California, 1994. Appliqué

Dutch Windows Lappendeken (detail of Quilt 28). Roberta Horton, Berkeley, California, 1994. Various Appliqué Stitches

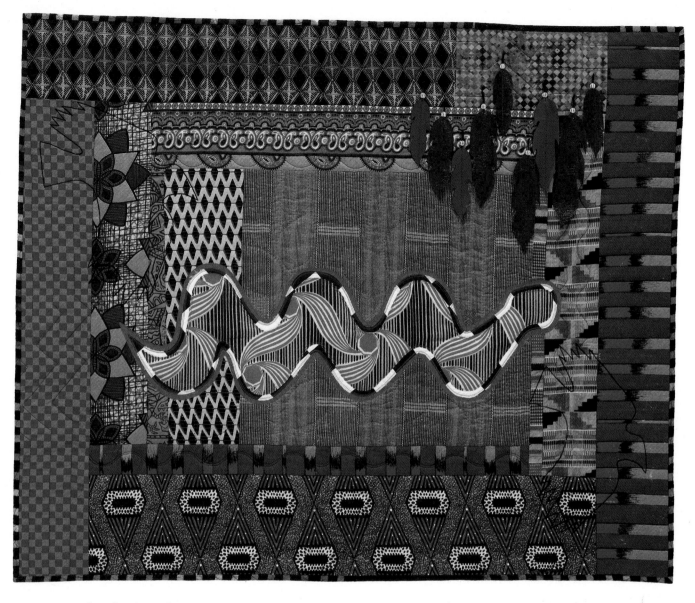

48. *No Cuervo.* 50" x 40". Judy Hopkins,
Anchorage, Alaska, 1994.

A small zigzag or other decorative stitch can be used in place of a straight stitch. Another idea is to sew first with a straight stitch to anchor the piece to the background, then go around a second time with a decorative stitch, perhaps using some of the new metallic and rayon threads. The choices are endless when you let your mind soar.

If you object to the raw-edge look, use a machine satin stitch, which overcasts the edge. It gives you both a wider and more densely sewn line than a zigzag stitch. It has long been used as a way to do machine appliqué. It gives the appearance of an outline, just like in a comic book.

Match the thread to the appliqué shape color if you want to soften the outline effect; contrast the thread color if you want to accentuate the outline feeling. Use a two-ply machine embroidery thread rather than regular three-ply sewing thread to get the smoothest stitching. I don't care for the stiff look of fusible webs so often used for satin stitch, so be sure you read the next section.

Machine Appliqué Recommendations

STRAIGHT STITCH, ZIGZAG, DECORATIVE, AND SATIN STITCH

1. Stiffen the appliqué shape with one of the following:
   a. A wash-away fabric stabilizer such as Perfect Sew™. Follow the directions on the bottle. Work on aluminum foil or wax paper to avoid messing up your work surface. Wash in luke-warm water to remove stiffness.
   b. Use spray starch; then iron.
2. Adhere appliqué shape to background:
   a. Hand baste.
   b. Dab on wash-away fabric stabilizer; heat set in place with iron.
   c. Use fabric glue stick sparingly to attach appliqué shape to background.
3. The background fabric usually also must be stabilized to prevent puckering and tunneling as you stitch. This is always true for satin stitch. I use a tear-away stabilizer on the underneath side of the background fabric. It's literally torn away when you have completed the stitching. There are several brands and weights so experiment until you find the one that you like. The product may vary with the selected stitch and the weight of the background fabric.
4. Use an open-toe presser foot if you're doing a satin, zigzag, or decorative stitch. This allows you to see what you're doing.
5. Using the right needle type and size can make a big difference. I work only with Schmetz needles. You will have to do some experimenting with your machine, the various types and brands of thread, and the fabric that you're using. Someone else can be using the exact same model as your machine, with identical fabric and thread as yours, and come up with different results. It must have something to do with how fast you sew and how you position and move your hands—even how you're holding your mouth.

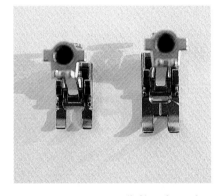

Open Toe Presser Foot (left) and Regular Presser Foot (right)

A few years ago sewing-machine needle makers discontinued the needle that we had all used for years and substituted something called a Universal, which is a semi-ballpoint needle. The lightly rounded point separates rather than pierces the threads, which produces a slightly angled stitch. The industry considers this the desired stitch as it doesn't damage the fabric. If you have wondered why your stitching doesn't look as straight as it used to, this is the reason.

My personal preference from years of sewing is that I like straight stitches that are uniform. A lot of my sewing is still done on my Singer Featherweight™ for this reason. A machine that only sews straight can deliver a true straight stitch. A zigzag machine won't. I switched to a Jeans/Denim 80/12 needle, which has an acute round point that will pierce the fabric to give a straight stitching line. This is my basic, all-purpose needle.

Now we have some other machine needle choices. A Quilting needle has a sharper point than the Jeans/Denim. A Top Stitching needle has a larger eye, which causes less friction on metallics. An Embroidery needle somehow helps to lay in two-ply thread smoothly.

Sewer's Aid is a silicone-like product. It can lubricate the thread to prevent breaking and fraying as it travels through your machine. It's a must for metallic threads. You may even find it helpful if you sew rapidly with rayon threads.

Application of Sewer's Aid

Suggestions for Threads

TYPE	NEEDLE	OTHER COMMENTS
1. Regular sewing (3-ply)	Denim 80/12, 70/10 Quilting 75/11	
2. Invisible nylon	Denim 80/12, 70/10 Quilting 75/11	Place thread in jar rather than on spindle
3. Machine embroidery (2-ply)	Embroidery 75/11 Denim 80/12 Universal 70/10	Lower top tension
4. Sulky® Rayon	Denim 80/12 Embroidery 75/11, 90/14 Topstitch 80/12, 90/14	Use Sewer's Aid if you sew fast
5. Metallic	Topstitch 90/14, 80/12 Embroidery 90/14, 75/11	May need to lower tension Use Sewer's Aid

Hand Appliqué

I have sewn appliqué by hand for years. I happen to use an Embroidery needle, size #8 or #9, because that's what my mom showed me to use years ago and they're easy to thread. Many appliqué artists use Quilting needles because they're smaller. The smaller the needle (the bigger the number), the smaller the stitch, so the rule goes. For some reason, Quilting needles continually unthread for me when I use one to do appliqué. If I do use a Quilting needle, I work with a #9. Some fanatical appliquérs use a size #12. I have large hands and that small size gets lost in my fingers. All I'm really saying is find a needle that fits your fingers and your eyes.

Serenity (detail of Quilt 37, page 79). Roberta Horton, Berkeley, California, 1993. Butterfly Appliqué

Pinning for Appliqué

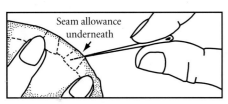

Sewing

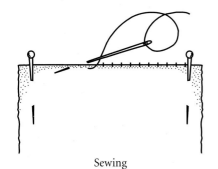

Seam allowance underneath

Convex Curves

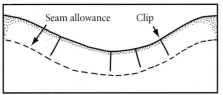

Seam allowance   Clip

Concave Curves

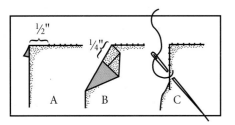

½"   ¼"

A   B   C

Right-Angle Corners

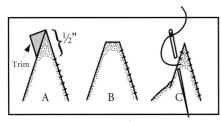

½"

Trim

A   B   C

Turning Corners With Sharp Points

Hassle-free Hand Appliqué:

1. Using an X or a straight line, baste shape to background. Don't bother to baste all around the edge.
2. Turn under the seam allowance (I prefer a skinny ¼") and hold it in place with pins placed perpendicular to the edge. Only work on a 2" to 3" section at a time. Do your pinning on a flat surface. Check the back periodically to see that you aren't creating puckers.
3. Use a hidden hemming stitch with thread matching the appliqué shape. Stitches should be about ⅛" apart. Be sure to pull thread snugly.
4. Convex curved areas (those that protrude out) will need some fullness eased in because you're turning a larger area into a smaller area. Turn under the seam allowance and feel for lumps. Place the piece flat on your worktable. Position your fingers on both sides of the lumpy area. Run the sharp end of a needle under the seam allowance, pulling gently up toward you. The tension created will allow you to redistribute the fullness. Pin. (Never clip this kind of curve!)
5. Concave curves (those that dip into the shape) may require clipping to release the tension as you turn under the seam allowance from a smaller area into a larger area. Cuts should be less than the ¼" seam allowance. Make a minimum of cuts; it's better to have to add more if the curve is still too tight. Make stitches closer together in this area.
6. Turning corners is done in three stages. Fold under the seam allowance to the end of one side, and trim any fabric that extends beyond the other side. Next, fold under a triangle at the tip; stitch to the point. Finally, fold under the second side's seam allowance. Put more stitches at corners to firmly anchor them.

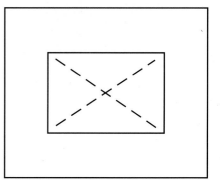

Hand Baste

Appliqué Patterns

Either you draw with ease, or not at all—or at least, with great reluctance. Children draw freely until their left brains take over in about the fourth grade and tell them they're not great artists. You have years of experience of trying to draw. You know what should, but doesn't, come out of the end of your pencil. So forget that pencil.

Instead, take up a pair of scissors. Most people haven't done much paper cutting since they gave up construction paper and paste in primary school. You don't have such a backlog of negative feelings about scissors. Because you don't know what you're doing, you'll find that you really can do it! All you need is a pad of unlined white paper (newsprint being the cheapest) and some scissors that both feel comfortable in your hand and that will cut paper. No eraser is necessary! The shape can come purely from you mind. Everyone can cut a recognizable butterfly. Or, you can use a design source to look at while you cut.

Paper Cutting With a Design Source

1. The plain piece of paper should be about the size you want the finished pattern to be. It may very well be a rectangle. Try to use the edges of the paper as a guide to size while you cut.

2. With the design source on a table in front of you, line up your eyes and your scissors with that design source. You will only be looking straight ahead, watching the perimeter of the design source. Start at the easiest point of entry. Make the first incision.

3. Continually turn the design source as you cut, keeping your eyes and scissors in line with the perimeter. Basically, you will only be making straight, or at the most, slightly curved cuts. The drawings here are an example of the turns that you would make to create a chicken shape. You will notice that the chicken starts out upside down because that seems to be the easiest place to enter the shape. The chicken's legs would be done as a second stage.

4. Don't be afraid to exaggerate and make something bigger as I did with my chicken feet in *Sangomas, Cocks, and Hens* (Quilt 21, page 49).

5. Now you have the basic outline of your pattern. Next, you will need to find fabric that fits your needs, realizing that the appliqué shape may change to fit the fabric (refer to the Visualizing in Fabric section of the Process chapter on page 48).

Turns Needed to Paper Cut Design

Design Source

Enlarging Method

Sometimes you find the perfect pattern that you would like to use but it's too small or too large. Rather than using a duplicating machine to change the size, I prefer to use the following grid method. It's available any time of the day, or night. I probably won't get a perfect copy but it will be good enough. The inaccuracies will make it more my own design.

1. Trace the proposed shape onto plain paper. Measure the widest part of the design. Using this measurement, form a square around the design. The square should touch the design on two sides. Cut out this square.

2. Make a second square the exact desired size of your design. Cut out this second square.

Draw Around Shape

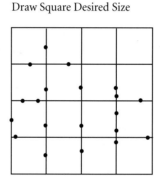

Draw Square Desired Size

3. Go through the following procedure with both paper squares: Fold each one in half, then repeat folding three more times so you end up with 16 equal divisions when each paper is opened. Draw with a ruler along the creases to form a grid on both squares.

4. Pay attention to the same division on both papers at one time. Put dots on the second paper where the drawing intersects the lines on the first paper. Starting in the upper left-hand corner of the second paper, move around the paper until all the necessary dots have been marked.

5. Always work in pencil and keep an eraser handy. Connect the dots to form the shape. If there is too much activity in one division, you may have to subdivide that square into a four-patch on both pieces of paper. This will give you a few more places for the design to intersect. You should now have an approximation of your desired shape.

6. Fine tune your design. Check for accuracy with the original. Sometimes the changes you accidentally made will actually look better.

7. Use the broad side of your pencil or a fat felt-tip marker to go around the outline. You will find this step vastly improves the result, since it tends to correct or smooth out lines. You now have an appliqué pattern. Don't forget to add the seam allowance if you're doing hand appliqué.

Place Dots Where Drawing Intersects Lines

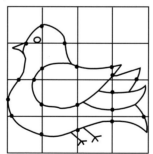

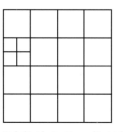

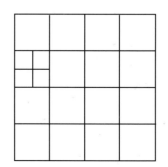

Subdivide in Complicated Areas

Quilting

Quilting seems to keep evolving and changing. Options multiply as new threads and batts become available. More quilters are trying machine quilting. And many are combining both hand and machine quilting in the same piece. It makes a lot of sense. Lynne Johnson had this to say about the quilting for *In the Face of Adventure* (Quilt 24, page 53): "I played with both hand and machine quilting and discovered that, to my surprise, I really like both in the same piece of work. For the most part, I let the fabric guide the quilting."

Whether you quilt by hand or by machine, I feel that the same criteria and suggestions can be applied. Often people just don't put in enough quilting, which can add a rich density to the finished project. It can be the most time-consuming part of making a quilt, but it's worth it.

For some reason, many people who machine quilt think that it requires less stitching than if the same piece were done by hand. Do they equate fast with sparse? This often results in large areas left unquilted, which can eventually sag—bereft of texture. I feel that adequate quilting helps a quilt to age well.

How do you decide what to quilt? Some things are obvious, such as going around the appliqué shapes. If the shape is big enough, you will need also to do some interior quilting. For this reason I carefully cut out the layers from behind the appliqués. I prefer to quilt on the background right next to the appliqué shape, which puffs it out. If you quilt on the appliqué edge, you'll have to stitch through several layers.

No Cuervo (detail). Judy Hopkins, Anchorage, AK, 1994. Mola-like outline done with machine appliqué quilting stitch

Some quiltmakers accomplish their appliqué and machine quilting in one step. The appliqué is secured to the background with basting or pins. As the quilting is stitched, it also goes through the appliqué shape. Judy Hopkins (Quilts 4, page 23, and 48, page 95), George Taylor (Quilts 16, page 43, and 31, page 67), and Susan Roberts (Quilt 49, page 104) used this technique.

I like to anchor all pieced seam lines, particularly the long ones. For hand quilting, this is done with matching cotton quilting thread, on the side of the seam without the seam allowance. When machine quilting, stitch with transparent (smoke) nylon quilting thread right in the seam. If the area is large enough to warrant more stitching, this may be done in a contrasting color. Light and medium solid-colored fabrics show the quilting the best. If the fabric is heavily patterned, you will only be able to achieve texture, so don't bother to try and execute complicated designs. You won't be able to see them.

When you're working with unusual fabrics, the answer is sometimes printed on the surface of the fabric itself. All you need to do is outline shapes or follow lines in the pattern. Ignore shapes that are too small or "dinky." You may find it advisable to quilt right over them as though the image didn't exist. Instead, pick out the larger elements to accentuate. Your quilting should flow rather than be spotty. Think of the shadows that will be cast. Also, I think in terms of enclosing shapes. Lines that end abruptly create wrinkles; those that encircle or flow into another shape present a more pleasing shadow.

The amount of quilting needs to be pretty consistent across the entire surface of the quilt. If one area is densely stitched, it will shrink up more than an adjacent area that doesn't have as much quilting. This causes the quilt to distort, which means it won't lie or hang straight. This often happens with stipple quilting, which is very densely stitched.

You can use the shrinking capability of quilting to your advantage. Sometimes one border is longer than the one opposite it or it ruffles due to excess fabric. A particular fabric can be more stretchy than the others used around it, causing an unsightly bubble. The answer to these predicaments is to simply add some more quilting. You may have heard the old proverb, "Just quilt it out!"

To audition quilting patterns, use a sheet of acetate (.005 thickness), which you can purchase in a tablet or roll at an art supply store. The clear film is designed for use in overlays, color separations, and layouts. I mark on the acetate with a water-soluble overhead projector pen; my favorite brand is Vis-à-Vis®.

Place the acetate over the area being considered. Make sure it extends beyond where you will be marking. (If you accidentally get the pen on your fabric, sponge out immediately with cold water.) Try drawing lines until you find something that works. You can "erase" inappropriate designs or mistakes on the acetate with a damp cloth or paper towel. This beats marking a proposed design with a pencil directly on the fabric, and then finding that you don't like it.

If you need to create a quilting motif to fill an area, refer back to the Appliqué section for information on paper cutting shapes (page 99) and enlarging (page 100). Once you have a satisfactory design, you're ready for the stitching. Many times actual lines don't have to be marked on the quilt top because the acetate serves as a reference on where to put the stitches. When guide lines are required, I mark them on the quilt as I'm working on an area. If needed, I make a template based on the acetate design, perfecting and refining it if necessary.

I tend to mark a quilt as I do the actual stitching. I have a drawer full of marking devices. The one I select for a particular project depends on the fabric itself (the color, value, and even the fabric weave) and the desired design. Here are my most frequently used tools:

1. A #2 pencil
2. A white Chaco-liner by Clover (chalk)
3. Fabric marking pencils like Clover Chacopel fine
4. ¼" masking tape (apply as needed, remove immediately)

Lorle Starling worked with a batt that required minimal machine quilting. Above is a detail of *African Impressions II: Sharing* (Quilt 22, page 51) after the first round of quilting where major divisions were quilted and appliqué shapes were outlined. What to add? The most challenging fabric design-wise was the hand-printed South African fabric on the bottom of the quilt. How would you quilt it? The lower photo is Lorle's answer. The acetate method was used to find the quilting design that suggests water flowing over the ferns and leaves. The answer was so clear and obvious once the pen touched the acetate; the solution seemed to appear like magic. Drawing the actual lines helps you to better visualize what the eventual quilting will look like.

Lorle added additional quilting in the upper mosaic background fabric. When she looked carefully, the divisions were already there. She also further defined the checkerboard with stitching. Wonderful stressed buttons were added to give more texture. Notice how they are attached.

African Impressions II: Sharing (detail of Quilt 22). Lorle Starling, Lake Oswego, Oregon, 1994. Minimal Quilting

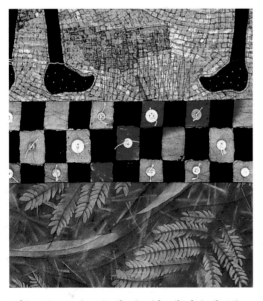

African Impressions II: Sharing (detail of Quilt 22). Additional Quilting and Button Embellishments

Lorle's finished quilt is on page 51. Many of the other solutions were printed right on the fabric. Lorle had used lots of fabrics that had printed subdivisions. Lorle's quilt came alive with the additional quilting. Don't be afraid to quilt the obvious. Going against the printed pattern can result in a confusing message for the viewer. Keep images as crisp and clear as possible.

Jerry Kelley truly works with an electric needle. She chose designs appropriate to each section of *Celebrate* (Quilt 1, page 18).

Joan Helm's stitching was generated by what was happening on the front of *Jambo Africa!* (Quilt 45, page 90). The use of Sulky rayon thread gave a beautiful shine to the stitches shown here. An interesting tracery of lines was superimposed across the women on the back of the quilt.

Judy Huddleston chose to hand quilt *Three Days and Thirteen Changes* (Quilt 13, page 40). Study the pattern of the background. She worked with straight lines that periodically changed direction. Placing the lines diagonally gives a feeling of movement.

Louise Colbert has miles of wonderful hand quilting on Almost African (Quilt 47, page 92). Study her handwork. She reminded me of a statement I made, "Beginning quilters don't want to know how much quilting there can be on a quilt." Notice the repetition of three of the shapes from the printed fabric in the quilted border.

Celebrate (detail of Quilt 1). Jerry Kelley, Nederland, Texas, 1993. Sufficient Machine Quilting

Above: *Jambo Africa!* (detail of Quilt 45). Joan Capron Helm, Portland, Oregon, 1992. Free-form Machine Quilting

Below: *Jambo Africa!* (details of Quilt 45). Nancy Capron, Portland, Oregon, 1992. Quilting by Joan Helm. Back of Quilt With Tracery of Machine Quilting

African Tapestry (Quilt 15, page 42) by Christine Davis beautifully combines hand and machine quilting. Her creative period definitely lasted into the quilting stage. In the detail shown here, particularly notice the sky-area behind the roof tops, which is an example of the design rule: **"It's important that the line isn't straight."**

Susan Roberts did her quilting on *Celestial Safari* with a Gammill quilting machine. It is possible to do a piece 14' x 30" with the quilt flat. She says, "I feel like I have an empty canvas in front of me; this wonderful machine allows me to draw free-form with a needle. The concept of moving the needle with the quilt stationary (instead of the needle being stationary and the quilt moving) is an exciting step forward for my work. Free-form drawing allows such a wonderful creative flow! Once in a great while, I sketch out a rough design in chalk first, but usually I just let it flow!"

It's necessary to do some experimenting when you machine quilt with some of the new threads. Refer to the Thread Chart on page 97 for suggestions about threads, needles, and so forth.

Above: 49. *Celestial Safari.* 31" x 45". Susan E. Roberts, Cooper Center, Alaska, 1994.

Right: *African Tapestry* (detail of Quilt 15). Christine Davis, Redmond, Washington, 1993. Interesting Background Quilting

Embellishments

In order for our quilts to survive for the longest time in the best possible condition, conservationists recommend that we add no embellishments. If longevity isn't your primary concern, welcome to the fun of embellishments.

I heard Safela Potoro, of Bophuthatswana, South Africa, say that she liked "to beautify the surface of her appliqué." I decided that this was a perfect description for embroidery. It's also a wonderful way to describe embellishments that we feel inspired to add to our quilts.

Three Days and Thirteen Changes (detail of Quilt 13, page 40). Judy Huddleston, Portland, Oregon, 1994. Embroidery Blanket Stitch

Embroidery

Embroidery is probably the oldest form of embellishment seen on quilts. Judy Huddleston has worked with a sun shape. Notice her use of an embroidery blanket stitch, which is more decorative than functional because it doesn't overcast the edge of the gold circle. This line of stitching is also erratic, which reinforces the fact that the center circle isn't really in the middle. Even the black quilting stitches on the gold area carry forth this look. Each step of the process was creative, being inspired by what preceded it.

Nancy Candelo added embroidery to her tree in *Almost African* (Quilt 25, page 55). She tried three stitches before she found the one that clicked. Additional foliage was added to better integrate the elephant and tree into the quilt. There is also some beading on the plants.

Judy Hopkins had planned to make a raven quilt. Instead a snake insinuated itself and *No Cuervo* (Quilt 48, page 95) was born. As a tribute to the raven, Judy embroidered two birds onto the quilt. She used the stem stitch like a quilting stitch, going through all three layers.

Beading

I like bead embellishments that feel appropriate to a quilt. They should be an integral part of the composition as opposed to something just "pasted on." Care needs to be taken in the selection and placement of such "goodies." Couching a necklace in place on a quilt doesn't show much creativity. Dismantling that necklace and sewing it in specially selected spots requires thinking and planning. In fact, only part of the necklace might be appropriate. Don't feel obligated to use something just because you happen to own it.

Beads are time-consuming to sew onto a quilt but are very addictive. Often is heard the refrain, "Let me add just one more bead...." Beads come in a fantastic variety. I tend to like ones that will hug the quilt, as opposed to ones that are very three-dimensional. Remember that beads are made for jewelry, like necklaces. Many beads will be too chunky for use on a quilt.

Seed beads are a common bead to use. They come in a variety of sizes. The higher the number, the smaller the size of the bead—and the hole in the bead. The smaller beads tend to form the straightest lines. I found number 11 to be my favorite size. Numbers 8 and 10 tended to wobble on the quilt, while number 12 was too small to thread. Seed beads come in a rainbow of colors and in a variety of finishes. Some of your options include opaque, transparent, matte (dull), lustre, metallic, and lined.

I recommend attaching beads with Nymo® nylon thread. It comes in different sizes. I found that I had the best success with the O size, which is made

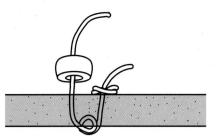

Knot Method A
1. Knot on top surface.
2. Two stitches on back.
3. Thread to front, and through bead (cover knot).

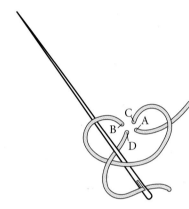

Knot Method B
1. Leaving a tail at A, make a tiny A-B stitch.
2. Take tiny C-D stitch, forming a loop.
3. Slip needle under and through loop; pull to knot. Clip tail.

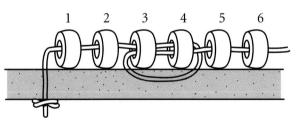

Seed Beads

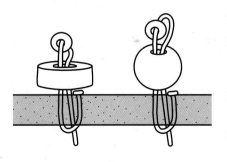

Large Flat or Round Beads

for use with seed beads. Other sizes are OO (the thinnest), B (a little thicker than O), and D (too thick to thread). The thread comes in various colors, such as white, black, brown, tan, blue, red, rust, and purple. Matching the thread to the quilt back helps when you want to hide the knot on the back. Sometimes the thread color is determined by the color of the bead and whether you want it to blend or contrast.

Very long beading needles, which have very small eyes, aren't required to sew beads onto a quilt. Use whichever needle you can both thread and get through the hole in the bead. A Sharp or a Quilting (Betweens) needle will work better than an Embroidery needle. For very tiny holes, you can try threading the bead itself. Or don't use the bead.

To keep your sanity, particularly with seed beads, place the beads in a container so they won't escape when you're trying to sew them. Lids to jars, box tops, small bowls and saucers will all work. The idea is to spear the bead with the needle rather than trying to place the bead on the needle with your fingers.

Beginning and ending knots are the $64,000 question. Everyone has a favorite method. Try to make them inconspicuous. Sometimes they can be placed on the front of the quilt and covered by the bead. If they must be left exposed on the back, use matching thread. Here are some suggested ways. Make sure that the beads are sewn on securely and snugly. Don't leave anything dangling as it is more likely to be accidentally ripped off of the surface. You will have to experiment for the shape and size of the bead that you're using.

Seed Beads (Retracing)
1. Knot on back and thread to front surface.
2. Stitch through beads #1, #2, #3, and #4.
3. Needle into quilt, retracing back to resurface between beads #2 and #3.
4. Stitch through beads #3 and #4, adding on the needle beads #5 and #6.
5. Needle into quilt. Follow sequence of stitching two previous sewn beads and adding two new beads.
6. Knot on back at end of sequence.

Large Flat or Round Beads
1. Knot on front surface (to be hidden under bead). Stitch to back of quilt, resurfacing on quilt front.
2. Sew through large bead, add smaller seed bead, stitch back through large bead.
3. Knot on back.

Ring-like Beads
1. Select contrasting color for thread as it will show and be a decorative element. Knot on back, stitch to front.
2. Come up on inside edge of bead. Bring thread over outside edge and stitch back into quilt. Resurface directly opposite, this time on the outside edge of the bead.
3. Stitch into center area, resurfacing on left outside edge.
4. Stitch into center, resurfacing on right outside edge. Stitch into center. Knot on back.

Warning: More care needs to be exercised when you handle an embellished quilt. Such quilts also weigh more.

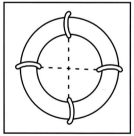

Ring-like Bead

Tracy Allen had her first beading experience on *Ester—A Tribal Star* (Quilt 9, page 34). She was inspired to try beading because the Ndebele women do intricate beadwork. Her lines of seed beads aren't straight, but I don't feel they need to be. Work on leather, which is stiffer than fabric, would give you straight lines. A careful look will reveal that some of the rows are merely the printed pattern of the fabric.

Left: *Ester—A Tribal Star* (detail of Quilt 9). Tracy Allen, Pacheco, California, 1993. Seed Bead Embellishments

Janet Shore has used a combination of beads to embellish *Stars of Africa* (Quilt 18, page 45). The mixture of yellow, orange, and rust beads helps to integrate the zebra circle into the background fabric. If only one color had been used, the beads would have isolated the circle from the background.

Charlene Phinney has used dimensional beads successfully on *Celebrating Freedom* (Quilt 34, page 69). The decorations are attached in a variety of creative ways, some using perle cotton. She's also couched some decorative yarns onto the quilt surface. Charlene says, "I had no set plan for the quilting and embellishments so they just came naturally. One area triggers an idea for a connecting area. The dancing figure on this quilt has really been an inspiration for future quilts. She not only is 'celebrating freedom,' but she has given me a renewed freedom in my quilts."

Left: *Stars of Africa* (detail of Quilt 18). Janet Shore, El Cerrito, California, 1994.

Below: *Celebrating Freedom* (detail of Quilt 34). Charlene Phinney, Puyallup, Washington, 1994. Beads Attached With Perle Cotton

Above: *Trois Poissons* (detail of Quilt 31). George Taylor, Anchorage, Alaska, 1994. Clear, Metallic Dull, and Metallic Shiny Beads

Above right: *Sterne* (detail of Quilt 16). George Taylor. Random Bead Placement

George Taylor used three different styles of seed beads on *Trois Poissons* (Quilt 31, page 67) clear, metallic dull, and metallic shiny. Each imparts a totally different feeling, providing a nice visual contrast on the surface of the quilt. On the above fish, he used various sizes and colors of flat discs held on with seed beads. He says, "I got into quite a beading frenzy!"

For *Sterne* (Quilt 16, page 43), George used a variety of different beads. Part of the fun of looking at the beaded decorations is to contrast the repetition in some areas and the variation in other sections. Even though George was working with a row of 12 printed diamonds, they're not all beaded the same way. The rhythm isn't every other one, either. Where it lends itself, don't always be predictable. Keep the viewers guessing—make them read the entire surface of the quilt.

Ruth Harris became a beading wizard on *Sunset in Nairobi* (details, page 109). She made the animals that she captured in free-hand cut Log Cabin blocks truly her own by lavishing them with beadwork. Ruth attached her beads with regular sewing thread and two-ply embroidery thread. The adornments were applied directly to the Log Cabin blocks, which were then attached to the quilt background. Quilting was done on a table, without a hoop.

Left and above: *Sunset in Nairobi* (details). Ruth Harris, Fairfax Station, Virginia, 1994.

Left: *Celebrating Freedom* (detail of Quilt 34). Charlene Phinney, Puyallup, Washington, 1994. Buttons Attached With Perle Cotton

Above: *In the Face of Adventure* (detail of Quilt 24). Lynne Johnson, West Linn, Oregon, 1994. Attaching Buttons

Buttons

Lynne Johnson used buttons on *In the Face of Adventure* (Quilt 24, page 53). You can see that there's more than one way to sew on a button. Six-strand embroidery floss can also be used to attach a button. This saves you the repeated motion of going back and forth through the holes of the button to anchor it. One trip through the holes does it.

Charlene Phinney tied some of her buttons with perle cotton (Quilt 34, page 69).

Sewing Hints

In most cases, beads, buttons, and found objects will have to be added to the project after it has been quilted. Ideally the process would be done while you're still working with the quilt top because then all the knots could be hidden inside the quilt. The answer will depend on whether you quilt by hand or machine, where the quilting stitches will go, whether or not a hoop is used, the location of the beading/buttons in concentrated areas or throughout the whole piece, and so forth.

Permanent Marking Pens

Permanent marking pens can be used to create or change a pattern. Alix Lee Bennett made animal designs directly on fabric. These were cut out and sewn on her quilt. She is one of the lucky few who can draw their own shapes with confidence. By the way, a permanent marking pen can also be used to fill in, mask over, or alter something that bothers you about a piece of fabric. I heat set when I'm finished with such "adjustments."

Cynthia Corbin is a quiltmaker and poet. She wrote one of her poems right on the front of her quilt, *Masks* (Quilt 3, page 22). She says, "I'm now into quilt top publishing!"

Fabric Paints

There are also a variety of fabric paints available for our use. Sue Arnold "improved" the design on her fabric. The red bird's wings read as too dark, so additional spots were added with a textile paint (Quilt 46, page 91).

Witch Doctor Healing Quilt (detail). Alix Lee Bennett, Los Gatos, California, 1994. Permanent Marking Pen Drawing

A Few Final Words

So, how can you be more creative as a quiltmaker? Let me count the ways…. Make each step of quiltmaking an adventure, a game. Don't be content with "safe" fabrics, but rather choose ones that send you down an exciting new pathway. Learn to listen to that challenging fabric. Experiment and try new solutions rather than staying with the tried-and-true. Listen to your inner thoughts; acknowledge your own creativity. You often have the answer—if you know how to pose the question.

BIBLIOGRAPHY

Inspiration Books:

Courtney-Clark, Margaret, *African Canvas: The Art of West African Women.* New York: Rizzoli International Publications, Inc., 1990.

Courtney-Clark, Margaret, *Ndebele: The Art of an African Tribe.* New York: Rizzoli International Publications, Inc., 1986.

Fauque, Claude, and Otto Wollenweber, *Tissus d'Afrique.* Paris: Syros-Alternatives, 1991.

Isaacs, Jennifer, *Australian Aboriginal Paintings.* Sydney, Australia: Weldon Publishing, 1989.

Liddell, Jill and Yuko Watanabe, *Japanese Quilts.* New York: E.P. Dutton, 1988.

Liddell, Jill with Patchwork Quilt Tsushin, *The Changing Seasons: Quilt Patterns from Japan.* New York: Dutton Studio Books, 1992.

Liddell, Jill, *The Story of the Kimono.* New York: E.P. Dutton, 1989.

Morris, Jean and Eleanor Preston-White, *Speaking with Beads: Zulu Arts from Southern Africa.* London: Thames and Hudson, 1994.

Oodgeroo, *Dreamtime: Aboriginal Stories.* New York: Lothrop, Lee & Shepard Books, 1994.

Segawa, Setsuko, *Japanese Quilt Art.* Kyoto, Japan: Mitsumura Suiko Shoin, 1985.

Segawa, Setsuko, *Japanese Quilt Art II: Progressive Quilt.* Kyoto, Japan: Mitsumura Suiko Shoin, 1987.

Sudo, Kumiko, *Expressive Quilts.* Berkeley, CA: Pegasus Publishing, 1989.

Technique Books:

Bawden, Juliet, *The Art and Craft of Appliqué.* London: Mitchell Beazley, 1992.

Hargrave, Harriet, *Heirloom Machine Quilting,* rev. ed. Lafayette, CA: C&T Publishing, 1990. (New revision, 1995)

Hargrave, Harriet, *Mastering Machine Appliqué.* Lafayette, CA: C&T Publishing, 1991.

Johnson, Vicki, *Paint and Patches.* Paducah, KY: American Quilter's Society, 1995.

Nilsson, Shirley, *Stitching Free: Easy Machine Pictures.* Lafayette, CA: C&T Publishing, 1993.

Noble, Maurine, *Machine Quilting Made Easy.* Bothell, WA: That Patchwork Place, 1994.

Buying Guide

The Cotton Patch
1025 Brown Avenue
Lafayette, California 94549
1-800-835-1177
(African, Japanese, and hand-dyed fabrics; reducing glasses)

Orb Weaver
4793 Telegraph Avenue
Oakland, California 94609
1-510-658-8131
(Beads; Nymo thread)

The publication of *The Fabric Makes the Quilt* marks the 25th anniversary of Roberta Horton's quiltmaking career. After learning to sew, knit, and embroider from her mother, Roberta continued her study of textiles through her B.S. degree in Home Economics from the University of California at Berkeley. After five years of public school teaching, Roberta retired and began her second career as a quiltmaker.

Combining her love of fabric with her love of teaching, Roberta taught the first state-accredited class in quiltmaking in California in 1973. Her personal goal was to teach, and eventually to write, disclosing what she had discovered about quiltmaking. This passion has taken Roberta to Japan, New Zealand, Australia, The Netherlands, Denmark, Germany, Norway, and South Africa as well as throughout the United States and Canada. Needless to say, she buys fabric in all of these places!

Roberta has previously authored four quiltmaking books. Her work has appeared in numerous quilt magazines and books. She designs plaids and stripes for Fasco/Fabric Sales of Seattle. Roberta recently was selected as one of the 88 most influential quiltmakers in the world by Nihon Vogue, publisher of *Quilts Japan*.

For information on workshops and lectures, write to Roberta Horton, 1929 El Dorado Avenue, Berkeley, California 94707-2404.

Other Fine Books From C&T Publishing:

An Amish Adventure, Roberta Horton
The Art of Silk Ribbon Embroidery, Judith Baker Montano
Beyond the Horizon, Small Landscape Appliqué, Valerie Hearder
Buttonhole Stitch Appliqué, Jean Wells
Dating Quilts: From 1600 to the Present, A Quick and Easy Reference, Helen Kelley
Elegant Stitches: An Illustrated Stitch Guide & Source Book of Inspiration, Judith Baker Montano
Faces & Places, Images in Appliqué, Charlotte Warr Andersen
Heirloom Machine Quilting, Harriet Hargrave
Impressionist Quilts, Gai Perry
Mariner's Compass Quilts, New Directions, Judy Mathieson
Paper Cuts and Plenty, Vol. III of Baltimore Beauties and Beyond, Elly Sienkiewicz
Schoolhouse Appliqué: Reverse Techniques and More, Charlotte Patera
Soft-Edge Piecing, Jinny Beyer
The Visual Dance: Creating Spectacular Quilts, Joen Wolfrom

For more information write for a free catalog from:
C&T Publishing
P.O. Box 1456
Lafayette, CA 94549
(1-800-284-1114)